How to
Master Skills for the

Second Edition

TOEFL® iBT

WRITING Intermediate

 DARAKWON

How to
Master Skills for the
Second Edition

TOEFL® iBT
WRITING Intermediate

Publisher Kyudo Chung
Editor Sangik Cho
Authors Michael A. Putlack, Will Link, Stephen Poirier
Proofreader Michael A. Putlack
Designers Minji Kim, Hyeonju Yoon

First Published in October 2007 By Darakwon, Inc.
Second edition first published in March 2025 by Darakwon, Inc.
Darakwon Bldg., 211, Munbal-ro, Paju-si, Gyeonggi-do 10881
Republic of Korea
Tel: 02-736-2031 (Ext. 250)
Fax: 02-732-2037

ISBN 978-89-277-8092-2 14740
        978-89-277-8084-7 14740 (set)

www.darakwon.co.kr

Photo Credits
Shutterstock.com

Components Main Book / Answer Key / Free MP3 Downloads
7 6 5 4 3 2 1   25 26 27 28 29

Table of
Contents

INTRODUCTION

1 Information on the TOEFL® iBT

A The Format of the TOEFL® iBT

Section	Number of Questions or Tasks	Timing	Score

Reading	**20 Questions**
	• 2 reading passages
	  – with 10 questions per passage
	  – approximately 700 words long each
		35 Minutes	30 Points

Listening	**28 Questions**
	• 2 conversations
	  – 5 questions per conversation
	  – 3 minutes each
	• 3 lectures
	  – 6 questions per lecture
	  – 3-5 minutes each
		36 Minutes	30 Points

Speaking	**4 Tasks**
	• 1 independent speaking task
	  – 1 personal choice/opinion/experience
	  – preparation: 15 sec. / response: 45 sec.
	• 2 integrated speaking tasks: Read-Listen-Speak
	  – 1 campus situation topic
	    reading: 75-100 words (45 sec.)
	    conversation: 150-180 words (60-80 sec.)
	  – 1 academic course topic
	    reading: 75-100 words (50 sec.)
	    lecture: 150-220 words (60-120 sec.)
	  – preparation: 30 sec. / response: 60 sec.
	• 1 integrated speaking task: Listen-Speak
	  – 1 academic course topic
	    lecture: 230-280 words (90-120 sec.)
	  – preparation: 20 sec. / response: 60 sec.
		17 Minutes	30 Points

Writing	**2 Tasks**
	• 1 integrated writing task: Read-Listen-Write
	  – reading: 230-300 words (3 min.)
	  – lecture: 230-300 words (2 min.)
	  – a summary of 150-225 words (20 min.)
	• 1 academic discussion task
	  – a minimum 100-word essay (10 min.)
		30 Minutes	30 Points

B What Is New about the TOEFL® iBT?

- The TOEFL® iBT is delivered through the Internet in secure test centers around the world at the same time.
- It tests all four language skills and is taken in the order of Reading, Listening, Speaking, and Writing.
- The test is about 2 hours long, and all of the four test sections will be completed in one day.
- Note taking is allowed throughout the entire test, including the Reading section. At the end of the test, all notes are collected and destroyed at the test center.
- In the Listening section, one lecture may be spoken with a British or Australian accent.
- There are integrated tasks requiring test takers to combine more than one language skill in the Speaking and Writing sections.
- In the Speaking section, test takers wear headphones and speak into a microphone when they respond. The responses are recorded and transmitted to ETS's Online Scoring Network.
- In the Writing section, test takers must type their responses. Handwriting is not possible.
- Test scores will be reported online. Test takers can see their scores online 4-8 business days after the test and can also receive a copy of their score report by mail.

2 Information on the Writing Section

The Writing section of the TOEFL® iBT measures test takers' ability to use writing to communicate in an academic environment. This section has two writing tasks. For the first writing task, you will read a passage and listen to a lecture and then answer a question based on what you have read and heard. For the second writing task, you will state and support an opinion in an online classroom discussion.

A Types of Writing Tasks

- **Task 1** Integrated Writing Task
  - You will read a short text of about 230-300 words on an academic topic for 3 minutes. You may take notes on the reading passage.
  - After reading the text, you will listen to a lecture discussing the same topic from a different perspective for about 2 minutes. You may take notes on the lecture.
  - You will have 20 minutes to write a 150-to-225-word summary in response to the question.

- **Task 2** Writing for an Academic Discussion Task
  - You will see a discussion board on a university website that comprises two students responding to a question posted by a professor.
  - You will have 10 minutes to read everything and to write a response to the topic in the online post. It should be at least 100 words.

B Types of Writing Questions

- Integrated Writing Task
  - Summarize the points made in the lecture, being sure to explain how they challenge specific claims/ arguments made in the reading passage.
    cf. *This question type accounts for almost all the questions that have been asked on the TOEFL® iBT so far.*
  - Summarize the points made in the lecture, being sure to explain how they cast doubt on specific points made in the reading passage.
  - Summarize the points made in the lecture, being sure to specifically explain how they answer the problems raised in the reading passage.

- Writing for an Academic Discussion Task
  - Yes or no questions: These questions require you to agree or disagree with a statement.
  - Preference questions: These questions ask you to state a preference between two similar things.
  - Open-Ended questions: These questions ask for your own thoughts or opinions on a broad topic.

C Important Features of Evaluation

- Quality of Response

  In the first task, the quality of the response is about how well you integrate and relate information from the reading and listening materials. In the second task, it is about the relevance and depth of your argument.

- Language Use

  Language use is about the accuracy and range of your grammar and vocabulary. In order to get good grades on the writing tasks, you should be able to use both basic and more complex language structures and choose the appropriate words.

HOW TO USE THIS BOOK

How to Master Skills for the TOEFL® iBT Writing Intermediate is designed to be used either as a textbook for a TOEFL® iBT writing preparation course or as a tool for individual learners who are preparing for the TOEFL® test on their own. With a total of sixteen units, this book is organized to prepare you for the test by providing you with a comprehensive understanding of the test and a thorough analysis of every question type. Each unit provides a step-by-step program that helps develop your test-taking abilities. At the back of the book are two actual tests of the Writing section of the TOEFL® iBT.

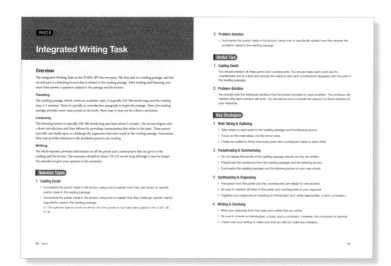

❶ Overview

This section is designed to prepare you for the type of task the part covers. You will be given a full sample question and a model answer in an illustrative structure.

❷ Note Taking & Vocabulary (Integrated Writing Task)

This section provides definitions of difficult words and phrases and also lets you take notes on the passages to make sure that you understand the main points in the passages.

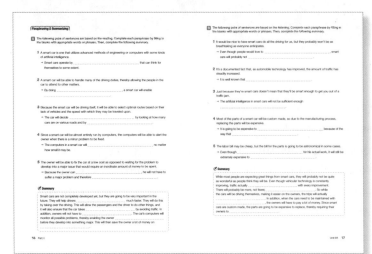

❸ Paraphrasing & Summarizing
(Integrated Writing Task)

This section provides you with the opportunity to paraphrase sentences from the reading and listening passages in order to improve your writing skills. There is also a summary of each passage in which words and phrases must be inserted to complete it.

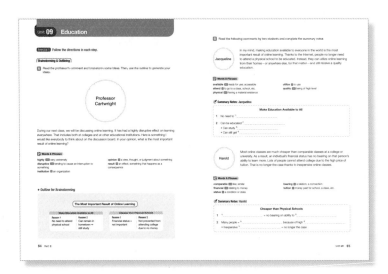

❹ Brainstorming & Outlining
(Writing for an Academic Discussion Task)

This section allows you to brainstorm about the professor's comments and has you complete two outlines to ensure that you understand the responses made by the students.

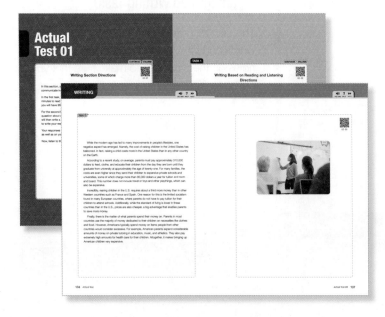

❺ Actual Test

This part will give you a chance to experience an actual TOEFL® iBT test. You will be given two sets of tests that are modeled on the Writing section of the TOEFL® iBT. The topics are similar to those on the real test, as are the questions. This similarity will allow you to develop a sense of your test-taking ability.

PART I

Integrated Writing Task

The integrated writing section consists of one task. You will be presented with a reading passage on a certain topic. Then, you will hear a lecture on the same topic. Typically, the lecture will have a position opposite that of the reading passage. Then, you will be asked a question in which you must write about the arguments made in the listening lecture and the reading passage. You will have 20 minutes to write an essay in response to the question. A typical essay is 150 to 225 words long.

Integrated Writing Task

Overview

The Integrated Writing Task on the TOEFL iBT has two parts. The first part is a reading passage, and the second part is a listening lecture that is related to the reading passage. After reading and listening, you must then answer a question related to the passage and the lecture.

Reading

The reading passage, which covers an academic topic, is typically 230-300 words long, and the reading time is 3 minutes. There is typically an introduction paragraph to begin the passage. Then, the reading passage provides some main points in the body. There may or may not be a short conclusion.

Listening

The listening lecture is typically 230-300 words long and takes about 2 minutes. The lecture begins with a short introduction and then follows by providing counterpoints that relate to the topic. These points typically cast doubt upon or challenge the arguments that were made in the reading passage. Sometimes they may provide solutions to the problems posed in the reading.

Writing

The ideal response provides information on all the points and counterpoints that are given in the reading and the lecture. The summary should be about 150-225 words long although it may be longer. You should not give your opinion in the summary.

Question Types

1 **Casting Doubt**

▸ Summarize the points made in the lecture, being sure to explain how they cast doubt on specific points made in the reading passage.

▸ Summarize the points made in the lecture, being sure to explain how they challenge specific claims/ arguments made in the reading passage.

cf. This question type accounts for almost all of the questions that have been asked on the TOEFL iBT so far.

2 Problem-Solution

▶ Summarize the points made in the lecture, being sure to specifically explain how they answer the problems raised in the reading passage.

Useful Tips

1 Casting Doubt

You should mention all three points and counterpoints. You should relate each point and its counterpoint one at a time and provide the reasons why each counterpoint disagrees with the point in the reading passage.

2 Problem-Solution

You should note the individual solutions that the lecture provides for each problem. The professor will mention why each solution will work. You should be sure to include the reasons for these solutions in your response.

Key Strategies

1 Note Taking & Outlining

▶ Take notes on each point in the reading passage and the listening lecture.

▶ Focus on the main ideas, not the minor ones.

▶ Create an outline to show how every point and counterpoint relate to each other.

2 Paraphrasing & Summarizing

▶ Do not repeat the words of the reading passage exactly as they are written.

▶ Paraphrase the sentences from the reading passage and the listening lecture.

▶ Summarize the reading passage and the listening lecture in your own words.

3 Synthesizing & Organizing

▶ Recognize how the points and the counterpoints are related to one another.

▶ Be sure to mention all three of the points and counterpoints in your response.

▶ Organize your response by including an introduction and, when appropriate, a short conclusion.

4 Writing & Checking

▶ Write your response from the notes and outline that you wrote.

▶ Be sure to include an introduction, a body, and a conclusion. However, the conclusion is optional.

▶ Check over your writing to make sure that you did not make any mistakes.

Directions Now you will see the reading passage for 3 minutes. Remember that it will be available to you again while you are writing. Immediately after the reading time ends, the lecture will begin, so keep your headset on until the lecture has ended.

Reading

One of the most controversial topics in education these days is the way to pay teachers their salaries. Many people favor determining teachers' salaries based on merit. In other words, teachers will be paid according to how well they teach and how well their students do in the classroom. This is an idea that should be implemented for a number of reasons.

First, this is a very fair way of paying teachers. Nowadays, teachers are paid primarily based upon seniority. The longer the person has been teaching, the more money the teacher receives. However, this is not fair. With the new method, the best teachers can receive the higher salaries they deserve even if they have not been teaching for very long. In addition, ineffective teachers will receive lower salaries even if they have been employed for ten or twenty years.

Second of all, paying teachers on a merit basis will encourage most of them to perform better. They will actually begin to compete with one another, which will improve the quality of the education they provide for their students. They will all improve when competing against one another. Likewise, they will start to develop better teaching methods in an effort to perform better in the classroom.

Finally, if the teachers are trying and working harder, then the students themselves will benefit greatly. The fact that the teachers are providing better lessons means that students will learn much better. The students themselves will also likely be inspired to study harder when they see just how hard their teachers are working.

It is obvious that a merit-pay-based system will have several benefits both for teachers and students. All school systems should consider implementing this method as soon as possible.

Listening

Now listen to part of a lecture on the topic you just read about.

01-01

Script

M Professor: I know that paying teachers based upon some sort of merit system sounds great. However, it actually has a number of disadvantages. You might not have considered them, so let me fill you in.

To begin with, who is going to determine the merit of each teacher? The principal, most likely. While most principals will do this in an honest fashion, some may not. First, the principal might use the merit-based policy to control many of the teachers. The teachers may have to follow the principal's rules or find their salaries getting cut. In addition, the principal may show favoritism toward various teachers and ignore good teachers instead to give pay raises to his friends. We can't allow that to happen.

Here's another point. Okay, yes, teachers will most likely try harder and develop new teaching methods and strategies. But they probably won't share any effective strategies with their colleagues. After all, they'll want to earn more money than them. This isn't what education should be about. Education is about sharing knowledge, not hoarding it. You're also likely to see less cooperation among teachers. All of this new competition is bound to create rivalries between faculty members.

Finally, this plan might have a negative effect on the students themselves. Since part of the merit-pay system will be determined by grades, teachers will be likely not to give failing or low grades to bad students. We'll probably see countless instances of grade inflation. Additionally, some teachers will probably pass students who should be kept back a grade. This will be doing the student a disservice and shouldn't happen.

As you can see, a merit-pay system would have a number of disadvantages. School systems should think hard before they implement them.

Directions You have 20 minutes to plan and write your response. Your response will be judged on the basis of the quality of your writing and on how well your response presents the points in the lecture and their relationship to the reading passage. Typically, an effective response will be 150 to 225 words.

 Summarize the points made in the lecture, being sure to explain how they cast doubt on the points made in the reading passage.

Sample Response

Introductory sentence The reading passage supports the idea of paying teachers according to how well they perform. **Topic sentence** However, the professor provides several reasons why merit pay is a bad idea.

Refutation 1 First of all, the professor claims that the principal will probably determine the merit of each teacher. He claims that some principals may be biased when they determine who the best and worst teachers are. He asserts that bad principals may force teachers to follow their rules or suffer poor evaluations. **Relation 1** Since the best teachers will get high salaries while the worst get low ones, he fears some principals may show favoritism to certain teachers when determining salaries.

Relation 2 Second, the professor acknowledges that teachers may try harder and develop better teaching methods. **Refutation 2** However, he doubts they will share their good methods with others. He says all the teachers will be competing against one another. He also believes there will be rivalries between teachers, so the overall quality of teaching might not rise.

Refutation 3 Finally, the professor thinks that teachers might not fail bad students. He also believes that teachers will harm the students by passing them when they should be failing them. Therefore, many students will not see positive benefits from the merit-pay system. **Relation 3** This point disproves the reading passage's contention that students will try harder when they see their teachers working hard.

Exercise Read, listen, and answer the question following each step.

Reading Read the following passage and take notes.

One of the most promising recent developments in personal transportation is the smart car. A smart car is one that utilizes advanced methods of engineering or computers with some kinds of artificial intelligence. While smart cars have not yet reached their full potential, they are sure to be beneficial to all who eventually drive them.

One advantage of smart cars is that they will help traffic flow faster. A smart car will be able to handle many of the driving duties, thereby allowing the people in the car to attend to other matters. Because the car, for the most part, will be driving itself, it will be able to select optimal routes based on their lack of vehicles and the speed with which they may be traveled upon. This, in turn, will make travel times much shorter and keep traffic moving continuously.

In addition, a smart car will have lower maintenance costs. Since the car will be almost entirely run by computers, the computers will be able to alert the owner when there is a minor problem to be fixed. The owner will then be able to fix the car at a low cost as opposed to waiting for the problem to develop into a major issue that would require an inordinate amount of money to be spent.

Words & Phrases

utilize v to use; to make use of
artificial adj not real; fake
potential v possibility
flow v to move; to pass by
attend to phr to take care of

optimal adj best; most favorable
maintenance n repair; preservation
alert v to warn; to tell someone about something
inordinate adj greater than normal; excessive

Note Taking

Smart Cars - Promising New Developments

1 Will help [1) _____
   • Handle many of the driving duties → drivers can attend to other matters
   • Can choose [2) _____ → much shorter travel times & continuously moving traffic

2 Have lower [3) _____
   • Computers will alert owner when is [4) _____
   • Can fix problem before it becomes major issue

Listen to a lecture on the topic you just read about and take notes.

✏ Note Taking

Smart Cars - Not As Breathtaking As People Anticipate

1 Will not ease traffic

- Automobile technology improves → 1) .... ↑
- People will have to sit in 2) ....

2 Will not be cheap to maintain

- Use of very expensive, 3) ....
- Replacing parts → 4) ....

01-02

🔍 **Words & Phrases**

thrilled adj very excited
breathtaking adj astonishing; wonderful; amazing
anticipate v to expect
zip v to move very quickly
unfortunately adv sadly

documented adj recognized; known
steadily adv at a regular pace
custom made adj specially built or made
labor v work
astronomical adj incredibly high; huge; very much

Comparing the Points Complete the main points from both notes as complete sentences.

Smart Cars

Reading (Main Points)	Listening (Refutations)
Smart cars will be able to select .... and avoid highly traveled roads, which will decrease .... for people.	Historically speaking, traffic always .... with each technological development; therefore, smart cars will still get stuck in ....
Because computers will warn the owners of ...., they can fix these problems while they are ...., which will not require a large amount of money.	Since many of the parts are ...., they have to be manufactured specially, so the cost of replacing them will be .... than normal.

A The following pairs of sentences are based on the reading. Complete each paraphrase by filling in the blanks with appropriate words or phrases. Then, complete the following summary.

1 A smart car is one that utilizes advanced methods of engineering or computers with some kinds of artificial intelligence.

→ Smart cars operate by _____ that can think for themselves to some extent.

2 A smart car will be able to handle many of the driving duties, thereby allowing the people in the car to attend to other matters.

→ By doing _____, a smart car will enable _____.

3 Because the smart car will be driving itself, it will be able to select optimal routes based on their lack of vehicles and the speed with which they may be traveled upon.

→ The car will decide _____ by looking at how many cars are on various roads and by _____.

4 Since a smart car will be almost entirely run by computers, the computers will be able to alert the owner when there is a minor problem to be fixed.

→ The computers in a smart car will _____ no matter how small it may be.

5 The owner will be able to fix the car at a low cost as opposed to waiting for the problem to develop into a major issue that would require an inordinate amount of money to be spent.

→ Because the owner can _____, he will not have to suffer a major problem and therefore _____.

✍ Summary

Smart cars are not completely developed yet, but they are going to be very important in the future. They will help drivers _____ much faster. They will do this by taking over the driving. This will allow the passengers and the driver to do other things, and it will also ensure that the car takes _____ by avoiding traffic. In addition, owners will not have to _____. The car's computers will monitor all possible problems, thereby enabling the owner _____ before they develop into something major. This will then save the owner a lot of money on _____.

B The following pairs of sentences are based on the listening. Complete each paraphrase by filling in the blanks with appropriate words or phrases. Then, complete the following summary.

1 It would be nice to have smart cars do all the driving for us, but they probably won't be as breathtaking as everyone anticipates.

→ Even though people would love to _____, smart cars will probably not _____.

2 It's a documented fact that, as automobile technology has improved, the amount of traffic has steadily increased.

→ It is well known that _____.

3 Just because they're smart cars doesn't mean that they'll be smart enough to get you out of a traffic jam.

→ The artificial intelligence in smart cars will not be sufficient enough

_____.

4 Most of the parts of a smart car will be custom made, so due to the manufacturing process, replacing the parts will be expensive.

→ It is going to be expensive to _____ because of the way that _____.

5 The labor bill may be cheap, but the bill for the parts is going to be astronomical in some cases.

→ Even though _____ for his actual work, it will still be extremely expensive to _____.

✒ Summary

While most people are expecting great things from smart cars, they will probably not be quite as wonderful as people think they will be. Even though vehicular technology is constantly improving, traffic actually _____ with every improvement. There will probably be more, not fewer, _____. So while the cars will be driving themselves, making it easier on the owners, the trips will actually _____. In addition, when the cars need to be maintained with _____, the owners will have to pay a lot of money. Since smart cars are custom made, the parts are going to be expensive to replace, thereby requiring their owners to _____.

Synthesizing | The following sentences are some important points from both the reading and the listening. Combine each pair of sentences to create your own sentence by using the given pattern.

1 **Reading** Because the car, for the most part, will be driving itself, it will be able to select optimal routes based on their lack of vehicles and the speed with which they may be traveled upon.

Listening It's a documented fact that as automobile technology has improved, the amount of traffic has steadily increased.

Combine The reading passage claims that ....

.... ,

but the professor claims that ....

....

2 **Reading** The smart car will make travel times much shorter and keep traffic moving continuously.

Listening While we may have cars do the driving for us, you can expect to sit in longer traffic jams.

Combine The author declares that ....

.... ,

yet the professor states that ....

....

3 **Reading** Smart cars will have lower maintenance costs.

Listening The fact that most parts are custom made means that due to the manufacturing process, replacing the parts will be expensive.

Combine In contrast to the statement in the reading claiming that ....

.... ,

the professor asserts that ....

....

4 **Reading** The owner will be able to fix the car at a low cost as opposed to waiting for the problem to develop into a major issue that would require an inordinate amount of money being spent.

Listening The labor bill may be cheap, but the bill for the parts is going to be astronomical in some cases.

Combine Whereas the reading passage asserts that ....

.... ,

the professor declares that ....

....

Organization   Review the notes from the reading and the listening. Complete the following chart with complete sentences.

Introduction	**1** The reading passage and the lecture both discuss ....
	2 However, the professor states that ....
	3 She gives two reasons why ....
Body 1	**4** First, the professor asserts that ....
	5 She states that as automobile technology has improved, ...
	6 This contradicts the reading passage, which affirms that ....
	7 In addition, the professor claims that ....
Body 2	**8** Next, the professor mentions ....
	9 She declares that ....
	10 The reading states that ....
	11 However, the professor states that while labor fees will not be expensive, ...
Conclusion (Optional)	**12** In conclusion, ...

Reading

One of the most promising new developments in personal transportation is the smart car. A smart car is one that utilizes advanced methods of engineering or computers with some kinds of artificial intelligence. While smart cars have not yet reached their full potential, they are sure to be beneficial to all who eventually drive them.

One advantage of smart cars is that they will help traffic flow faster. A smart car will be able to handle many of the driving duties, thereby allowing the people in the car to attend to other matters. Because the car, for the most part, will be driving itself, it will be able to select optimal routes based on their lack of vehicles and the speed with which they may be traveled upon. This, in turn, will make travel times much shorter and keep traffic moving continuously.

In addition, a smart car will have lower maintenance costs. Since the car will be almost entirely run by computers, the computers will be able to alert the owner when there is a minor problem to be fixed. The owner will then be able to fix the car at a low cost as opposed to waiting for the problem to develop into a major issue that would require an inordinate amount of money to be spent.

Listening

✎ Note Taking

01-02

Q Summarize the points made in the lecture, being sure to explain how they cast doubt on specific points made in the reading passage.

──

──

──

──

──

──

──

──

──

──

──

──

──

──

──

──

──

──

──

Self-Evaluation Check your response by answering the following questions.

	Yes	No
1 Are all the important points from the lecture presented accurately?	☐	☐
2 Is the information from the lecture appropriately related to the reading?	☐	☐
3 Is the response well organized?	☐	☐
4 Are all the sentences grammatically correct?	☐	☐
5 Are all the words spelled correctly?	☐	☐
6 Are all the punctuation marks used correctly?	☐	☐

Exercise Read, listen, and answer the question following each step.

Reading Read the following passage and take notes.

Many environmentalists are wary of allowing the introduction of new species into an ecosystem. Ecosystems are fragile, and exotic species can often cause many problems when they are introduced where they do not belong. In fact, when they invade a new ecosystem, they frequently have several harmful effects.

For one, the introduction of new species can ruin the local ecosystem in many ways. First, it can act as a predator and eat other local species, thereby causing their extinction. Another way is that it can consume too much of a valuable local food source. This consumption can cause other animals not to be able to eat as much as they are accustomed to. The result may be a decrease in the number of native species.

Another way that nonnative species can be harmful is by causing the people who live in that area to suffer from financial losses. An example of this is the mesquite tree in the American Southwest. It thrives in areas with little water. However, because it soaks up the water from the ground, nearby grasses do not get enough and die. This causes local ranchers to lose money since they have to pay extra for animal feed. In addition, the mesquite tree regenerates easily, so farmers must pay large amounts of money to remove the trees from their land.

Words & Phrases

wary of phr cautious about; suspicious of
fragile adj easily destroyed or broken
invasive adj moving into a place where one does not belong
ruin v to destroy

predator n an animal that kills and eats other animals
consume v to eat; to take in
be accustomed to phr to be used to
thrive v to prosper
regenerate v to grow back; to renew

Note Taking

Exotic Species - Harmful to the Environment

1 Ruin the local ecosystem
   • Can be a predator and [1) _____ → make them become extinct
   • Can consume too many natural resources → native species do not have [2) _____

2 Cause local individuals to suffer financial losses → e.g. mesquite trees
   • [3) _____ from the ground → grasses die from a lack of water
   • [4) _____ → farmers must pay a lot of money to remove the trees

Listening Listen to a lecture on the topic you just read about and take notes.

✎ Note Taking

Exotic Species - Not Always Harmful

01-03

1 Do not harm their new ecosystems
- 1) _____ in Kansas ➜ has not caused any species to go extinct
- 2) _____ in Texas ➜ have not killed any native species

2 Can be beneficial ➜ e.g. 3) _____
- Devours many insects ➜ keeps the bug population down
- Farmers do not need 4) _____ ➜ poisons will not hurt humans

---

📖 Words & Phrases

detrimental adj harmful

beneficial adj helpful; useful

celebrated for phr famous for

extinction n the act of dying out; the death of a species

wildlife n animals

excessive adj too much

graze v to eat grass in a field

harmless adj not harmful or dangerous; innocuous

devour v to eat completely

pesticide n a poison that kills insects

Comparing the Points Complete the main points from both notes as complete sentences.

Exotic Species

Reading (Main Points)	Listening (Refutations)
Exotic species can _____ by killing all the native species or by _____.	Many exotic species, like _____, do not have any negative effects on their new ecosystems because they do not _____.
Some nonnative species like _____ can cause _____ because of its killing of local plant life or the cost of paying for its removal.	Some exotic species, like _____, which kills bugs and keeps farmers from _____ that can be harmful to humans, can actually be helpful to people.

A The following pairs of sentences are based on the reading. Complete each paraphrase by filling in the blanks with appropriate words or phrases. Then, complete the following summary.

1 Ecosystems are fragile, and exotic species can often cause many problems when they are introduced where they do not belong.

→ When _____ go to a new place, they can often cause many problems because _____ .

2 An exotic species can act as a predator and eat other local species, thereby causing their extinction.

→ Some nonnative species _____ , occasionally to the point of _____ .

3 The fact that exotic species eat all of the food can cause other animals not to be able to eat as much as they are accustomed to.

→ Some native species _____ because exotic species are _____ .

4 Another way that nonnative species can be harmful is by causing the people who live in that area to suffer from financial losses.

→ Some exotic species are detrimental because _____ .

5 The mesquite tree regenerates easily, so farmers must pay large amounts of money to remove the trees from their land.

→ It is expensive _____ from a plot of land since they _____ .

✎ **Summary**

Because ecosystems can _____ , most environmentalists do not want animal or plant species introduced to a new area. For example, exotic species might act as _____ and kill all of a local species. Or they might simply eat _____ , which will cause these animals to starve to death. Other exotic species cause _____ . An example of this is the mesquite tree. This tree kills all the local grass, so farmers need to purchase more food for their animals. The trees are also hard to _____ , so farmers have to spend a lot of money paying for their removal.

B The following pairs of sentences are based on the listening. Complete each paraphrase by filling in the blanks with appropriate words or phrases. Then, complete the following summary.

1 Although we've discussed a lot of harmful exotic species, please remember that they are not always detrimental to the local ecosystem.

→ While many exotic species _____, this is not always the case.

2 Everyone knows that Kansas is famous for wheat and that Texas is celebrated for cows.

→ It is well known that _____.

3 Cows are not predators, so no animals have been killed by them while they graze.

→ Cows are harmless creatures that _____.

4 A perfect case of a beneficial exotic species is that of the cane toad, which was introduced for farmers down in Florida, among other places.

→ The cane toad in Florida, one of the places the animal was introduced,

_____.

5 Since the toads eat so many insects, farmers don't have to use any pesticides that could be dangerous to humans.

→ Because cane toads _____, there is no need to

_____.

✏ Summary

Many people believe that all exotic species harm their new environments, but that is not necessarily true. Some nonnative plants and animals do not _____.
Two examples of this are _____. The wheat has never killed another local species. Likewise, the cows simply graze in their fields and do not harm others. In addition, some exotic species can actually _____.
_____ is one such example. It kills many insects that eat farmers' crops. Its presence also means that farmers do not have to resort to using _____ on their crops. In this case, the cane toad has truly improved the local environment.

The following sentences are some important points from both the reading and the listening. Combine each pair of sentences to create your own sentence by using the given pattern.

1 **Reading** First, a nonnative species can act as a predator and eat other local species, thereby causing their extinction.

Listening For example, wheat has not caused the extinction of any local wildlife.

Combine The reading declares that ....

.... ,

but the professor claims that ....

....

2 **Reading** Another way is that exotic species can consume too much of a valuable local food source.

Listening And cows, of course, are not predators, so no animals have been killed by them while they graze.

Combine While the author of the reading passage claims that ....

.... ,

the professor states that ....

....

3 **Reading** The mesquite tree's killing of local grasses causes local ranchers to lose money since they have to pay extra for animal feed.

Listening Cane toads devour many harmful insects, so they keep the bug population down.

Combine In opposition to the claim that ....

.... ,

the professor asserts that ....

....

4 **Reading** In addition, the mesquite tree regenerates easily, so farmers must pay large amounts of money to remove the trees from their land.

Listening In addition, since the toads eat so many insects, farmers don't have to use any pesticides that could be dangerous to humans.

Combine Contrasting the reading's assertion that ....

.... ,

the professor believes that ....

....

Review the notes from the reading and the listening. Complete the following chart with complete sentences.

Introduction	**1** The reading passage and the lecture are both about _____ , but they disagree as to _____ .
	2 The professor believes that _____ .
	3 However, the reading passage believes _____ .
Body 1	**4** The professor first states that _____ .
	5 He claims that _____ .
	6 The reading, however, disagrees and claims that _____ .
	7 In addition, they sometimes eat all of an area's food supply, which _____ .
Body 2	**8** The professor also asserts that _____ .
	9 He cites the example of _____ .
	10 He claims that _____ .
	11 However, the reading claims that _____ .
	12 The reading states that since mesquite trees kill grass, _____ .
	13 It is also expensive to _____ .
Conclusion (Optional)	**14** Clearly, _____ .

Reading

Many environmentalists are wary of allowing the introduction of new species into an ecosystem. Ecosystems are fragile, and exotic species can often cause many problems when they are introduced where they do not belong. In fact, when they invade a new ecosystem, they often have several harmful effects.

For one, the introduction of new species can ruin the local ecosystem in many ways. First, it can act as a predator and eat other local species, thereby causing their extinction. Another way is that it can consume too much of a valuable local food source. This consumption can cause other animals not to be able to eat as much as they are accustomed to. The result may be a decrease in the number of native species.

Another way that nonnative species can be harmful is by causing the people who live in that area to suffer from financial losses. An example of this is the mesquite tree in the American Southwest. It thrives in areas with little water. However, because it soaks up the water from the ground, nearby grasses do not get enough and die. This causes local ranchers to lose money since they have to pay extra for animal feed. In addition, the mesquite tree regenerates easily, so farmers must pay large amounts of money to remove the trees from their land.

Listening

✎ Note Taking

01-03

Q Summarize the points made in the lecture, being sure to explain how they cast doubt on specific points made in the reading passage.

Self-Evaluation Check your response by answering the following questions.

	Yes	No
1 Are all the important points from the lecture presented accurately?	☐	☐
2 Is the information from the lecture appropriately related to the reading?	☐	☐
3 Is the response well organized?	☐	☐
4 Are all the sentences grammatically correct?	☐	☐
5 Are all the words spelled correctly?	☐	☐
6 Are all the punctuation marks used correctly?	☐	☐

Exercise Read, listen, and answer the question following each step.

Reading Read the following passage and take notes.

    A contentious issue in American politics is whether or not to raise the gasoline tax. Many people support it because they believe it will help the economy. However, their beliefs are erroneous since raising the gas tax would definitely have negative effects on the economy.

    To begin with, an increase in the gas tax would disrupt the economy. Many people rely upon their cars to get to work. By raising the gas tax just a few percentage points, the government would be making people's commutes to work cost more. In many cases, they cannot afford this extra expense. In addition, if people are spending more money on gasoline, then they will spend less money purchasing other products. Since the American economy runs on consumer spending, a decrease in spending could greatly damage the economy.

    Second of all, an increase in the gasoline tax would hurt those with low incomes. Naturally, it would make their gasoline more expensive, and these people simply do not have the money they would need to pay the tax. Additionally, since many people with low incomes live in areas with no public transportation, they might not be able to afford to go out or even make it to their workplaces. At best, they would suffer increased financial hardship.

Words & Phrases

contentious adj controversial; causing disagreement
erroneous adj incorrect; wrong; misleading
rely upon phr to depend on
commute n the trip from one's home to one's workplace
run on phr to need; to depend on

hurt v to harm; to damage
income n wages; earnings
transportation n ways to move from one place to another
make it phr to get somewhere in time
hardship n difficulty

Note Taking

Raising the Gasoline Tax - A Bad Economic Idea

1 Would disrupt the economy
- Could hurt [1] _____ → make it difficult to afford commuting to work
- People spend less on other products → could damage [2] _____

2 Would hurt people with low incomes
- Gasoline becomes [3] _____ → poor people cannot afford it
- No [4] _____ → people cannot get to work or go out

Listen to a lecture on the topic you just read about and take notes.

Note Taking

Raising the Gasoline Tax - No Harm to the Economy

01-04

1 Would not disrupt the economy
- Economy is 1) _____ → gasoline tax cannot hurt it
- Other factors are damaging economy → 2) _____ and infrastructure

2 Can help poor people
- Give 3) _____ to people with low incomes
- Charge less at 4) _____ → people with low incomes save money

Words & Phrases

touchy adj sensitive

refer to phr to speak about; to mention

disrupt v to interfere with

complex adj complicated; intricate

dramatically adv severely; significantly; radically

tremendous adj very large

infrastructure n a transportation network

affect v to influence

tax break n relief from paying higher taxes

rebate n a repayment; a refund

Comparing the Points Complete the main points from both notes as complete sentences.

Raising the Gasoline Tax

Reading (Main Points)	Listening (Refutations)
Increasing the gasoline tax would be bad for America because it would increase the prices of _____ and also _____, which would harm the economy.	A rise in the gasoline tax would not hurt the economy since _____ to be affected by it and also because there are other problems like _____ that are causing economic damage.
Raising the gasoline tax would harm people with low incomes since they would not be able to _____ and do not have access to good _____ .	While a gasoline tax would hurt people with low incomes, the government could give them _____ or _____ for gasoline at gas stations.

Paraphrasing & Summarizing

A The following pairs of sentences are based on the reading. Complete each paraphrase by filling in the blanks with appropriate words or phrases. Then, complete the following summary.

1 Their beliefs are erroneous since raising the gas tax would definitely have negative effects on the economy.

→ People who think .... are wrong.

2 By raising the gas tax just a few percentage points, the government would be making people's commutes to work cost more.

→ If ...., it will make

.... for everyone.

3 If people are spending more money on gasoline, then they will spend less money purchasing other products.

→ .... will cause people to

....

4 Raising the gasoline tax would make gasoline more expensive, and people with low incomes simply do not have the money they would need to pay the tax.

→ People who .... would not be able to afford gas

if ....

5 Since many people with low incomes live in areas with no public transportation, they might not even be able to afford to go out or even make it to their workplaces.

→ Those with low salaries who .... will not have

enough money to ....

✒ Summary

Although some people believe the government should increase the gasoline tax, it would actually

.... First, many people use their cars to drive to work. Raising

the gas tax would make these trips .... And then people

would spend less money .... The American economy needs

people to buy things, or else it will start getting bad. In addition, a high gasoline tax would be bad

for people who .... They might not even be able to afford to

.... Since they cannot take public transportation, it would be

difficult for them to get around.

B The following pairs of sentences are based on the listening. Complete each paraphrase by filling in the blanks with appropriate words or phrases. Then, complete the following summary.

1 I must say that I'm strongly in favor of raising the gas tax for a number of reasons.

→ In my view, there are many reasons _____.

2 Our economy is way too complex for just one factor to hurt the economy.

→ Due to _____, one factor alone cannot

_____.

3 There are many other factors, like health care and fixing the nation's infrastructure, that are already doing tremendous economic damage.

→ Many other things, such as _____, are already

harming the economy.

4 The government could give tax breaks to people whose incomes are below a certain level.

→ The government could _____ on people who

_____.

5 The government could also allow people with lower incomes to pay less money when they go to fill up their cars.

→ It might be possible to _____.

✐ Summary

The professor fully supports _____ for a couple of different
reasons. First, he does not agree with arguments that a higher gas tax would harm the economy.
Since the American economy is so _____, it would be impossible
for an increased gas tax to damage it. Likewise, issues like _____
are already causing lots of damage to the economy. Second, while people with
_____ would be hurt by an increased tax, there are ways to avoid
this pain. The government could give them _____ to compensate
them for the increase in taxes. Or they could simply pay less when they go to fill up their cars.

The following sentences are some important points from both the reading and the listening. Combine each pair of sentences to create your own sentence by using the given pattern.

1 **Reading** By raising the gas tax just a few percentage points, the government would be making people's commutes to work cost more.

Listening For one thing, our economy is way too complex for just one factor to hurt the economy.

Combine The reading passage declares that ....
.... ,
but the professor claims that ....
....

2 **Reading** In addition, if people are spending more money on gasoline, then they will spend less money purchasing other products.

Listening There are also many other factors, like healthcare expenses and fixing the nation's infrastructure, that are already doing tremendous economic damage.

Combine The reading claims that ....
.... ,
yet the professor argues that ....
....

3 **Reading** Naturally, it would make their gasoline more expensive, and these people simply do not have the money they would need to pay the tax.

Listening For example, the government could give tax breaks to people whose incomes are below a certain level.

Combine In response to the claim that ....
.... ,
the professor states that ....
....

4 **Reading** Additionally, since many people with low incomes live in areas with no public transportation, they might not even be able to afford to go out or even make it to their workplaces.

Listening Or the government could also allow people with lower incomes to pay less money when they go to fill up their cars.

Combine While the reading asserts that ....
.... ,
the professor maintains that ....
....

Organization Review the notes from the reading and the listening. Complete the following chart with complete sentences.

Introduction	1 The professor firmly disagrees with the reading passage, which states that .... 2 Instead, the professor feels that ....
Body 1	3 To begin with, the reading passage declares that .... 4 The author also mentions that .... 5 Since the American economy ...., it would start to go into decline. 6 However, the professor believes .... 7 Plus, a gas tax's effects cannot compare to ...., which are already damaging the current economy.
Body 2	8 The reading also states that .... 9 The professor mentions that .... 10 He also thinks that ....
Conclusion (Optional)	11 The professor and the reading passage ....

Reading

A contentious issue in American politics is whether or not to raise the gasoline tax. Many people support it because they believe it will help the economy. However, their beliefs are erroneous since raising the gas tax would definitely have negative effects on the economy.

To begin with, an increase in the gas tax would disrupt the economy. Many people rely upon their cars to get to work. By raising the gas tax just a few percentage points, the government would be making people's commutes to work cost more. In many cases, they cannot afford this extra expense. In addition, if people are spending more money on gasoline, then they will spend less money purchasing other products. Since the American economy runs on consumer spending, a decrease in spending could greatly damage the economy.

Second of all, an increase in the gasoline tax would hurt those with low incomes. Naturally, it would make their gasoline more expensive, and these people simply do not have the money they would need to pay the tax. Additionally, since many people with low incomes live in areas with no public transportation, they might not be able to afford to go out or even make it to their workplaces. At best, they would suffer increased financial hardship.

Listening

> ✎ Note Taking

01-04

Q Summarize the points made in the lecture, being sure to explain how they cast doubt on specific points made in the reading passage.

_____

_____

_____

_____

_____

_____

_____

_____

_____

_____

_____

_____

_____

_____

_____

_____

_____

_____

Self-Evaluation Check your response by answering the following questions.

	Yes	No
1 Are all the important points from the lecture presented accurately?	☐	☐
2 Is the information from the lecture appropriately related to the reading?	☐	☐
3 Is the response well organized?	☐	☐
4 Are all the sentences grammatically correct?	☐	☐
5 Are all the words spelled correctly?	☐	☐
6 Are all the punctuation marks used correctly?	☐	☐

Exercise Read, listen, and answer the question following each step.

Reading Read the following passage and take notes.

Because of the dangers of forest fires, some park rangers have started promoting a new way to take care of forests. Their method is called prescribed burning. What they do is actually start fires in forests to burn down various kinds of trees or other plant life. Unfortunately, prescribed burning is not an effective method for a number of different reasons.

First, fires are extremely difficult to control. While park rangers insist that they take tremendous precautions, it is still possible for a prescribed burn to rage out of control. This has actually happened in some cases. Because the rangers could not control the fire, it caused much more damage than a regular forest fire would have. In fact, fire is unpredictable. Rangers may want to burn one area but instead end up burning additional places because of the unpredictability of forest fires.

In addition, prescribed burning is not cheap. It costs a large amount of money to start and control a forest fire. There are numerous people and machines involved in this process, so salaries and equipment costs must be paid. Moreover, when fires start burning uncontrollably, it costs even more money to reign them back in. All things considered, prescribed burning has many disadvantages and should not be practiced.

Words & Phrases

promote v to support; to endorse
prescribed adj arranged; managed
insist v to claim; to state
tremendous adj great; very large
precaution n a safety measure
rage v to burn

unpredictable adj random; unknown
end up V-ing phr to wind up V-ing
numerous adj a lot of; a large number of
reign something back in phr to get something back in control

Note Taking

Prescribed Burning - An Ineffective Alternative to Forest Fires

1 Difficult to control

- Can rage out of control → can burn more areas than [1)] ....
- [2)] .... → may start to burn other unintended places

2 Very expensive

- Must pay for [3)] ....
- Can cost more when fires begin [4)] ....

Listening | Listen to a lecture on the topic you just read about and take notes.

Note Taking

Prescribed Burning - An Effective Alternative to Forest Fires

01-05

1 Rangers handle the fires
- Can control exactly [1] ________________ & determine which trees and plants to burn
- Have ways to ensure fires do not [2] ________________

2 Helps rejuvenate forests
- Natural fire → [3] ________________ as damaging as prescribed fire & can burn homes and kill people
- Can keep fires on [4] ________________

Words & Phrases

recover v to get better; to go back to normal
uncontrollably adv wildly
handle v to take care of
expert n a specialist; a professional
consult v to discuss with; to check with
commence v to begin; to start
ensure v to make sure; to guarantee
rejuvenate v to invigorate; to enliven
settlement n a place where people live
authority n a person in control or power

Comparing the Points | Complete the main points from both notes as complete sentences.

Prescribed Burning

Reading (Main Points)	**Listening** (Refutations)
Some prescribed burning fires may get ________________, which makes them burn more land than was planned and makes them ________________ to control.	________________ consult experts to make sure that their fires do not burn out of control, and if the fires ________________, they have ways to make sure the fires do not become very bad.
Prescribed burning is not cheap because ________________ must be paid, and it becomes ________________ if the fire starts to burn out of control.	Prescribed burning can cause much less damage than ________________ and can help a forest ________________ by burning only a small part of it.

Paraphrasing & Summarizing

A The following pairs of sentences are based on the reading. Complete each paraphrase by filling in the blanks with appropriate words or phrases. Then, complete the following summary.

1 Prescribed burning is not an effective method for a number of different reasons.

→ There are a lot of reasons why _____.

2 While park rangers insist that they take tremendous precautions, it is still possible for a prescribed burning to rage out of control.

→ Despite the fact that park rangers claim _____, a prescribed burning can still suddenly _____.

3 Rangers may want to burn one area but instead end up burning additional places because of the unpredictability of forest fires.

→ Sometimes unpredictable forest fires _____ that the park rangers did not _____.

4 It costs a large amount of money to start and control a forest fire.

→ _____ can be expensive.

5 When fires start burning uncontrollably, it costs even more money to reign them back in.

→ It can become more expensive to _____ once it starts to _____.

✎ Summary

Prescribed burning is the practice of starting forest fires _____
and controlling them so that they burn a small area of the forest. This method, however,
has some disadvantages. The first disadvantage is that the fires can sometimes
_____. Fires are hard to control, and some prescribed
burnings have actually gotten out of control and burned unintended places. In fact,
rangers often wind up _____ because they cannot control
the fires. The second disadvantage is the cost involved. Paying people's salaries and
_____ is expensive. In addition, when the fires get out of control, it
costs a lot of money to _____.

B The following pairs of sentences are based on the listening. Complete each paraphrase by filling in the blanks with appropriate words or phrases. Then, complete the following summary.

1 Some environmentalists actually believe that starting forest fires is effective.

→ According to certain environmentalists, _____ .

2 Park rangers are able to manage exactly where the fire burns and even what plants and trees it burns down.

→ Park rangers can _____ that they know which areas will burn and _____ .

3 Even if the fire starts burning unpredictably, park rangers have methods to ensure that the fire does not get out of their control and burn the wrong places.

→ Rangers know _____ if it should start burning unpredictably and _____ .

4 Natural forest fires can cause up to ten times the damage prescribed burning does.

→ Prescribed burnings _____ .

5 By using prescribed burning, authorities can control exactly what gets burned while keeping the fire on a small scale.

→ Prescribed burning enables rangers to _____ while not allowing the fire to _____ .

Summary

The professor claims that prescribed burning actually has a number of positive benefits. The first one he cites is that _____ are able to control these prescribed burnings. Because they consult with experts, they know exactly how to _____ . In addition, if there is a case where the fire starts to get out of their control, they know a number of different _____ . Second of all, the professor claims that natural forest fires _____ the damage that prescribed burnings do. Natural fires also often damage homes and kill people. However, prescribed burnings can take place on _____ , burn down unwanted areas, and help the forest rejuvenate.

Synthesizing The following sentences are some important points from both the reading and the listening. Combine each pair of sentences to create your own sentence by using the given pattern.

1 **Reading** While park rangers insist that they take tremendous precautions, it is still possible for prescribed burnings to rage out of control.

Listening Park rangers are able to manage exactly where the fire burns and even what plants and trees it burns down.

Combine In contrast to the reading passage's claim that ....

.... ,

the professor insists that ....

....

2 **Reading** Rangers may want to burn one area but instead end up burning additional places because of the unpredictability of forest fires.

Listening Even if the fire started burning unpredictably, they have methods to ensure that the fire does not get out of their control and burn the wrong places.

Combine The author of the reading passage writes that ....

.... ,

yet the professor states that ....

....

3 **Reading** It costs a large amount of money to start and control a forest fire.

Listening However, natural forest fires can cause up to ten times the damage prescribed burning does and also get into human settlements, burn down houses and other buildings, and even kill people.

Combine The author of the writing declares that .... ;
however, the professor counters that claim by stating that ....

....

4 **Reading** Additionally, when fires start burning uncontrollably, it costs even more money to reign them back in.

Listening By using prescribed burning, authorities can control exactly what gets burned while keeping the fire on a small scale.

Combine The reading passage states that ....

.... ,

but the professor insists that ....

....

Organization Review the notes from the reading and the listening. Complete the following chart with complete sentences.

Introduction	1 The professor claims that _____ _____, yet the reading passage declares the opposite.
	2 The professor gives several reasons to _____ _____.
Body 1	3 First, in contrast to the claim that _____, the professor says that _____.
	4 He also claims that _____ _____.
	5 In addition, the professor states that _____ _____.
	6 This is countered by the reading assertion that _____ _____.
Body 2	7 Second, the professor declares that _____ _____.
	8 Meanwhile, the reading says that _____ _____.
	9 The reading also states that _____ _____.
	10 However, the professor mentions that _____ _____.
Conclusion (Optional)	11 The professor and the reading clearly disagree with one another with regard to _____.

Reading

Because of the dangers of forest fires, some park rangers have started promoting a new way to take care of forests. Their method is called prescribed burning. What they do is actually start fires in forests to burn down various kinds of trees or other plant life. Unfortunately, prescribed burning is not an effective method for a number of different reasons.

First, fires are extremely difficult to control. While park rangers insist that they take tremendous precautions, it is still possible for a prescribed burn to rage out of control. This has actually happened in some cases. Because the rangers could not control the fire, it caused much more damage than a regular forest fire would have. In fact, fire is unpredictable. Rangers may want to burn one area but instead end up burning additional places because of the unpredictability of forest fires.

In addition, prescribed burning is not cheap. It costs a large amount of money to start and control a forest fire. There are numerous people and machines involved in this process, so salaries and equipment costs must be paid. Moreover, when fires start burning uncontrollably, it costs even more money to reign them back in. All things considered, prescribed burning has many disadvantages and should not be practiced.

Listening

✎ Note Taking

01-05

Q Summarize the points made in the lecture, being sure to explain how they cast doubt on specific points made in the reading passage.

_____
_____
_____
_____
_____
_____
_____
_____
_____
_____
_____
_____
_____
_____
_____
_____
_____
_____
_____
_____

Self-Evaluation Check your response by answering the following questions.

	Yes	No
1 Are all the important points from the lecture presented accurately?	☐	☐
2 Is the information from the lecture appropriately related to the reading?	☐	☐
3 Is the response well organized?	☐	☐
4 Are all the sentences grammatically correct?	☐	☐
5 Are all the words spelled correctly?	☐	☐
6 Are all the punctuation marks used correctly?	☐	☐

Exercise Read, listen, and answer the question following each step.

Reading Read the following passage and take notes.

These days, many schools and research institutions find themselves relying more and more upon educational DVDs and computer videos. While some purists, preferring to use books, are vehemently against this trend, the reliance upon visual materials is actually a positive thing.

First of all, educational materials are useless if the audience does not pay attention to them. The twenty-first century is a visual age. Students are much more used to watching DVDs and computer videos than to reading books. By relying upon visual aids, educators are more likely to capture the attention of students. In addition, DVDs and computer videos are more easily able to explain difficult processes and ideas through the use of graphics and computer animation. This quality makes difficult topics much easier to understand, a definite merit that will help students further their education.

DVDs and computer videos are also much cheaper than books. Many visual aids sell for fewer than ten dollars while books may cost two or three times that amount. Since many students are on tight budgets, this economic benefit will help them considerably. Additionally, many schools only have to purchase one DVD or computer video as opposed to buying thirty or forty or more copies of the same book. By purchasing visual materials, schools can save considerable amounts of money, which they can use to buy other important materials.

📖 Words & Phrases

purist ⓝ a traditionalist; a person opposed to change
vehemently adv passionately; very strongly
reliance ⓝ dependence
visual adj related to sight
capture the attention of phr to cause someone to pay attention

process ⓝ a method; a way
merit ⓝ an advantage
on a tight budget phr without much money to spend
considerably adv significantly; greatly
purchase ⓥ to buy
as opposed to phr instead of

✎ Note Taking

Educational Visual Aids - Effective Educational Tools

1　21st century = a visual age
- Students - used to ¹⁾ _____ → help capture their attention
- DVDs and computer videos - explain concepts with ²⁾ _____
  → easier to understand

2　Are not expensive
- Are much cheaper than books → good for students on ³⁾ _____
- Schools can ⁴⁾ _____ → use money on other purchases

Listen to a lecture on the topic you just read about and take notes.

Note Taking

Educational Visual Aids - Not As Good As People Believe

01-06

1 Provide limited information

- Are incomplete because of [1)] ....
- Are designed for entertainment ➜ cannot explain difficult topics & are [2)] ....

2 Are not really cheaper

- [3)] .... ➜ expensive ($50-100)
- Must purchase DVD player and TV or computer ➜ additional expenses of [4)] ....

Words & Phrases

inform [v] to tell
educate [v] to teach; to inform
limit [v] to restrict
impart [v] to provide; to convey
contain [v] to have; to include

design [v] to construct; to create
simplified [adj] shortened; made easier
pricey [adj] expensive
annoying [adj] bothersome

Comparing the Points
Complete the main points from both notes as complete sentences.

Educational Visual Aids

Reading (Main Points)	Listening (Refutations)
Educational visual aids can both .... and .... by using computer graphics or animation.	Visual aids often provide limited information due to ...., and they typically rely upon ....
Visual aids are ...., which can be helpful to students on tight budgets, and schools only need ...., so they can spend their money on other necessities.	Educational visual aids can be .... than books and also require expensive DVD players and TVs or computers, equipment that can sometimes ....

Paraphrasing & Summarizing

A The following pairs of sentences are based on the reading. Complete each paraphrase by filling in the blanks with appropriate words or phrases. Then, complete the following summary.

1 While some purists, preferring to use books, are vehemently against this trend, the reliance upon visual materials is actually a positive thing.

→ Despite the fact that _____, they are actually beneficial to use.

2 By relying upon visual aids, educators are more likely to capture the attention of students.

→ Teachers can _____ if they

_____.

3 DVDs and computer videos are more easily able to explain difficult processes or ideas through the use of graphics and computer animation.

→ Since they use graphics and animation, visual aids can _____

_____.

4 Many visual aids sell for fewer than ten dollars while books may cost two or three times that amount.

→ The prices of books _____.

5 By purchasing visual materials, schools can save considerable amounts of money, which they can use to buy other important materials.

→ Because schools will _____ by purchasing visual aids, they can use the money to _____.

✒ Summary

The use of _____ like DVDs and computer videos is something positive even though some people oppose them. The first reason given is that most students are used to watching videos instead of reading books. Therefore, teachers can _____ more easily. These visual aids can also make difficult concepts _____ by using graphics and animation. Second of all, the prices of visual aids are much lower than those of books. This is good for students _____ and for schools since the schools can buy just one DVD or computer video and use the leftover money for _____.

B The following pairs of sentences are based on the listening. Complete each paraphrase by filling in the blanks with appropriate words or phrases. Then, complete the following summary.

1 I must inform you that books are still much better than watching visual aids.

→ It is preferable to _____.

2 The video is likely to be incomplete and not contain all the necessary information.

→ Visual materials _____.

3 Visual materials are often designed more for entertainment than education.

→ Entertaining, not educating, is _____.

4 DVDs and computer videos are often rather cheap, but this isn't the case for educational materials.

→ Educational visual materials are _____.

5 Even if you own the DVD, you still have to purchase the DVD player and the television set or the computer, which aren't cheap.

→ Without _____, you cannot watch a DVD.

✎ **Summary**

The professor feels that _____ is a much preferable alternative to watching visual materials like DVDs and computer videos. First, she states that visual materials often provide _____ because they have to be so short. Books, on the other hand, hold much more information. Visual materials also tend to simplify things since they are more interested in _____ instead of educating them. In addition, the professor says that books are actually cheaper than DVDs and computer videos. The reason is that _____ can be much more expensive than movies. Finally, a person with a DVD needs to purchase _____ or a computer, which will cost more money to keep up.

Synthesizing The following sentences are some important points from both the reading and the listening. Combine each pair of sentences to create your own sentence by using the given pattern.

1 **Reading** By relying upon visual aids, educators are more likely to capture the attention of students.

Listening Therefore, the video is likely to be incomplete and not contain all the necessary information.

Combine The author of the reading declares that ....

.... ;

however, the professor counters by saying that ....

....

2 **Reading** In addition, DVDs and computer videos are more easily able to explain difficult processes and ideas through the use of graphics and computer animation.

Listening In addition, visual materials are often designed more for entertainment than education.

Combine The reading mentions that ....

.... ,

yet the professor believes ....

....

3 **Reading** Many visual aids sell for fewer than ten dollars while books may cost two or three times that amount.

Listening Educational visual aids are almost always very pricey, costing between fifty to one hundred dollars.

Combine In contrast to the reading, which states that ....

.... ,

the professor claims that ....

....

4 **Reading** By purchasing visual materials, schools can save considerable amounts of money, which they can use to buy other important materials.

Listening In addition, even if you own the DVD, you still have to purchase the DVD player and the television set or the computer, which aren't cheap.

Combine While the reading passage mentions that ....

.... ,

the professor states that ....

....

Review the notes from the reading and the listening. Complete the following chart with complete sentences.

Introduction	1 The professor declares that ....
	2 This is in direct contrast to the reading passage, which claims ....
Body 1	3 First, the professor states that ....
	4 She says that videos are only a couple of hours long, so ....
	5 The author of the reading, meanwhile, claims that ....
	6 The reading also states that ....
	7 The professor, however, says that ....
Body 2	8 Second of all, the professor declares .... while the reading claims the opposite.
	9 In addition, the professor says that .... , yet the reading claims ....
	10 The reading further says that ....
	11 But the professor states that ....
Conclusion (Optional)	12 The professor and the reading passage stand on opposite sides of the debate over ....

Reading

These days, many schools and research institutions find themselves relying more and more upon DVDs and computer videos. While some purists, preferring to use books, are vehemently against this trend, the reliance upon visual materials is actually a positive thing.

First of all, educational materials are useless if the audience does not pay attention to them. The twenty-first century is a visual age. Students are much more used to watching DVDs and computer videos than to reading books. By relying upon visual aids, educators are more likely to capture the attention of students. In addition, DVDs and computer videos are more easily able to explain difficult processes and ideas through the use of graphics and computer animation. This quality makes difficult topics much easier to understand, a definite merit that will help students further their education.

DVDs and computer videos are also much cheaper than books. Many visual aids sell for fewer than ten dollars while books may cost two or three times that amount. Since many students are on tight budgets, this economic benefit will help them considerably. Additionally, many schools only have to purchase one DVD or computer video as opposed to buying thirty or forty or more copies of the same book. By purchasing visual materials, schools can save considerable amounts of money, which they can use to buy other important materials.

Listening

🖉 Note Taking

01-06

Q Summarize the points made in the lecture, being sure to explain how they cast doubt on specific points made in the reading passage.

_____

_____

_____

_____

_____

_____

_____

_____

_____

_____

_____

_____

_____

_____

_____

_____

_____

_____

_____

_____

_____

Self-Evaluation Check your response by answering the following questions.

	Yes	No
1 Are all the important points from the lecture presented accurately?	☐	☐
2 Is the information from the lecture appropriately related to the reading?	☐	☐
3 Is the response well organized?	☐	☐
4 Are all the sentences grammatically correct?	☐	☐
5 Are all the words spelled correctly?	☐	☐
6 Are all the punctuation marks used correctly?	☐	☐

Exercise Read, listen, and answer the question following each step.

Reading Read the following passage and take notes.

In recent years, companies have begun noticing that a large percentage of their employees are not waiting until their sixties to retire. Instead, they are opting for early retirement and are leaving the workforce while they are still in their fifties. After conducting several studies, companies have recognized a couple of reasons for this sudden spate of early retirements by their employees.

To begin with, many employees who are in their fifties have been working for the same employer and doing the same jobs for many years or even decades. What happens is that they simply become burned out from doing the same tasks over and over again. Furthermore, they discover that their daily routines are no longer challenging but have instead become incredibly boring for them.

Second of all, many older people compare themselves with their company's younger employees. When this comparison happens, the results are typically not favorable. Older employees are just unable to maintain the same pace as younger ones; therefore, the older individuals see themselves accomplishing less work than their younger colleagues. In addition, older workers begin to feel as if they are a burden on the company and are not contributing as much as they could. This self-accusing feeling then encourages them to depart their company and to take early retirement.

Words & Phrases

notice v to see; to observe
retire v to stop working, usually because of one's age
opt for phr to choose; to select
workforce n personnel; manpower
spate n an increase; a wave
decade n a period of ten years

burned out phr exhausted; worn out
favorable adj positive
maintain v to keep
burden n a weight; an onus
contributing adj helping; assisting

Note Taking

Early Retirement of Employees in Their Fifties

1 Have worked for the same company for many years
   • Become [1) ....] from doing their jobs
   • Discover their [2) ....] are boring

2 Compare themselves with younger employees
   • [3) ....] than younger ones
   • Feel like they are [4) ....]

Listen to a lecture on the topic you just read about and take notes.

Ways to Ensure Elderly Employees' Usefulness

01-07

1 Give them part-time jobs

- Would not have to come in every day ➡ won't [1)] ....
- Will have fresh minds ➡ won't [2)] ....

2 Utilize their experience

- Provide them with [3)] ....
- Consult them more often ➡ makes them [4)] .... & can draw upon their experience

Words & Phrases

underutilize [v] to use less than one should

elderly [adj] old; aging

population [n] the number of people living in a certain area

be willing to-V [phr] to want to-V

accomplish [v] to achieve

worn out [adj] extremely tired or exhausted

a range of [phr] various; a variety of

task [n] a job

consult [v] to discuss with; to talk with

draw upon [phr] to use; to utilize

Comparing the Points
Complete the main points from both notes as complete sentences.

Early Retirement for Elderly Employees

Reading (Problems)	Listening (Solutions)
Employees at the same jobs for many years become .... and also .... by doing the same tasks again and again.	It is recommended that companies hire elderly employees on a .... to keep them from becoming too .... and to keep them interested in their work.
Older employees believe that they .... than younger employees and therefore feel they are	Companies need to utilize .... by giving them various tasks and also by .... on a more regular basis.

A The following pairs of sentences are based on the reading. Complete each paraphrase by filling in the blanks with appropriate words or phrases. Then, complete the following summary.

1 In recent years, companies have begun noticing that a large percentage of their employees are not waiting until their sixties to retire.

→ Nowadays, it has come to companies' attention that ....
....

2 Many employees who are in their fifties have been working for the same employer and doing the same jobs for many years or even decades.

→ .... have remained employed by their companies and are made to do the same tasks for ....

3 What happens is that older employees simply become burned out from doing the same tasks over and over again.

→ Doing the same jobs repeatedly makes older workers ....
....

4 Many older people compare themselves with their company's younger employees.

→ Elderly employees are often ....

5 Older employees are just unable to maintain the same pace as younger ones; therefore, the older individuals see themselves accomplishing less work than their younger colleagues.

→ The elderly have trouble ...., which gives them the feeling that ....

✒ Summary

Companies have long wondered why many of their workers began ....
as opposed to their sixties, and now they have a couple of reasons as to why. First, many elderly
employees .... after doing the same jobs day after day for
very long periods of time. They simply quit because they cannot handle the boredom of their
work. Second, elderly workers recognize that they are ....
by younger employees, which causes their opinions of their value to the company to decline.
Realizing they are not .... as they could be and that they are
.... their employers with their presence, they just quit their jobs.

B The following pairs of sentences are based on the listening. Complete each paraphrase by filling in the blanks with appropriate words or phrases. Then, complete the following summary.

1 I'd like to continue talking about how society underutilizes its elderly population.

→ Let me carry on with some examples as to _____.

2 A large number of elderly people would be willing to work part time.

→ Lots of older people would _____.

3 Letting the elderly work part time would keep their minds fresh, which means that they wouldn't become bored with their work.

→ By only working part time, _____.

4 I know all of you young people think that you know everything, but your experiences are nothing compared to those of a fifty- or sixty-year-old person.

→ Many people in their teens and twenties _____ in comparison to those more than twice their age.

5 Being consulted by the company would not only make elderly workers feel wanted but would also draw upon their many years of experience working at the company.

→ The effects of being consulted would be _____ and also _____ that have built up by their long years or employment.

✍ Summary

The professor believes that it is pointless for people in their fifties to retire and not work anymore, so she provides some suggestions to get people to _____.
She thinks that instead of working full time, elderly people should be allowed to
_____. This measure would keep the employees
_____ to do their jobs. In addition, companies should try to involve their elderly employees in more activities and ask them for _____
on various things. This effort would give elderly workers the confidence they require
and at the same time also help their companies by having them rely upon people with
_____.

Synthesizing The following sentences are some important points from both the reading and the listening. Combine each pair of sentences to create your own sentence by using the given pattern.

1 **Reading** What happens is that older employees simply become burned out from doing the same tasks over and over again.

Listening However, a large number would be willing to work part time.

Combine The author of the reading passage claims that ....

.... ,

so the professor suggests ....

....

2 **Reading** Furthermore, older employees discover that their daily routines are no longer challenging but have instead become incredibly boring for them.

Listening In addition, letting the elderly work part time would keep their minds fresh, which means that they wouldn't become bored with their work.

Combine The problem in the reading is that ....

.... ,

so the professor suggests that ....

....

3 **Reading** Older employees are just unable to maintain the same pace as younger ones; therefore, the older individuals see themselves accomplishing less work than their younger colleagues.

Listening For example, companies could give elderly employees a wider range of duties instead of making them repeat tasks over and over.

Combine In the reading, the author suggests that ....

.... ;

however, the professor suggests ....

....

4 **Reading** In addition, older workers begin to feel as if they are a burden on the company and are not contributing as much as they could.

Listening And the companies could consult with their elderly employees more often.

Combine The author of the reading passage mentions that ....

.... ,

so the professor mentions that ....

....

Review the notes from the reading and the listening. Complete the following chart with complete sentences.

Introduction	1 The reading passage mentions a couple of reasons as to .... 2 The professor provides a couple of solutions for ....
Body 1	3 The first problem the reading mentions is that .... 4 So the professor believes .... 5 In addition, working part time will keep the elderly from ....
Body 2	6 Another problem leading to early retirement is that .... 7 Therefore, the professor suggests that .... 8 Additionally, companies could consult elderly employees .... 9 By doing so, companies could make their older employees feel as though ....
Conclusion (Optional)	10 In conclusion, ...

Reading

In recent years, companies have begun noticing that a large percentage of their employees are not waiting until their sixties to retire. Instead, they are opting for early retirement and are leaving the workforce while they are still in their fifties. After conducting several studies, companies have recognized a couple of reasons for this sudden spate of early retirements by their employees.

To begin with, many employees who are in their fifties have been working for the same employer and doing the same jobs for many years or even decades. What happens is that they simply become burned out from doing the same tasks over and over again. Furthermore, they discover that their daily routines are no longer challenging but have instead become incredibly boring for them.

Second of all, many older people compare themselves with their company's younger employees. When this comparison happens, the results are typically not favorable. Older employees are just unable to maintain the same pace as younger ones; therefore, the older individuals see themselves accomplishing less work than their younger colleagues. In addition, older workers begin to feel as if they are a burden on the company and are not contributing as much as they could. This self-accusing feeling then encourages them to depart their company and to take early retirement.

Listening

✏ Note Taking

01-07

Q Summarize the points made in the lecture, being sure to specifically explain how they answer the problems raised in the reading passage.

Exercise Read, listen, and answer the question following each step.

Reading Read the following passage and take notes.

Nowadays, lots of universities are raising their students' tuition. In some cases, the raises are quite substantial. While many students are not pleased with these increases, there are some legitimate reasons for the hikes.

First, universities are constantly striving to upgrade their educational quality. Since fewer people are attending college these days, schools must fight for all the students they can get. One ideal way to attract students is to ensure that the school provides them with an outstanding education. Additionally, by increasing the school's academic rank, the school will attract both more students and better ones. Since it costs money to enhance the quality of education, the school's budget must increase. Therefore, tuition must also go up.

Second, many universities are finding themselves short of cash these days. This is particularly true of state universities, which often depend upon the state government for the majority of their budgets. Unfortunately, many states are cutting general funding to schools. Most particularly hard hit are the funds for the general management of the university. While not necessarily a glamorous job, it is crucial to the wellbeing of the school. Without sufficient general management funds, many schools would be facing serious problems, so they need to compensate for the lost funds in other ways. It is therefore obvious why schools are increasing tuition every year.

📖 Words & Phrases

substantial adj large; considerable
legitimate adj reasonable; justifiable; valid
hike n an increase; a raise
constantly adv continuously
strive v to struggle; to attempt

ensure v to guarantee
outstanding adj excellent; extremely good
enhance v to improve
compensate for phr to make up for
glamorous adj exciting; attractive

✏️ Note Taking

University Tuition Increases

1 Need to improve school to attract students
   • Must provide 1) .... → costs more money
   • Must increase 2) .... → need higher budget

2 Are often short of cash
   • 3) .... getting funding cut → must make up for lost cash
   • 4) .... losing funds → schools facing serious problems

Listen to a lecture on the topic you just read about and take notes.

Note Taking

Universities Don't Need Money to Raise Quality

01-08

1 Other ways to improve school
- Professors - lecture better and develop [1)] _____
- Students - [2)] _____ in and out of class

2 Ties with corporations
- Schools get [3)] _____ → useful to students and faculty
- Companies can [4)] _____ from school body

Words & Phrases

offset [v] to counterbalance
augment [v] to increase; to improve
tie [n] a connection
corporation [n] a company; a business
benefit [v] to profit
state-of-the-art [adj] modern; high-tech

faculty [n] the members of a teaching staff
the inside track [phr] an advantage
recruit [v] to employ; to hire
contribute to [phr] to assist; to help
win-win situation [phr] an occasion where both parties do well

Comparing the Points
Complete the main points from both notes as complete sentences.

University Tuition Increases

Reading (Problems)	Listening (Solutions)
Schools need more money to improve _____ and to increase the school's _____ if they want to attract more and better students.	In order to improve the school, professors can improve _____ while students can do better both in the classroom and _____ .
Schools are getting _____ cut as well as seeing less funding go to their general management, so they have to make up for this loss with _____ .	Schools should increase _____ so that they may receive exceptional free facilities while the corporations will be able to _____ who learned with those facilities.

A The following pairs of sentences are based on the reading. Complete each paraphrase by filling in the blanks with appropriate words or phrases. Then, complete the following summary.

1 While many students are not pleased with tuition increases, there are some legitimate reasons for these hikes.

→ .... even though schools have some good

reasons for ....

2 Since fewer people are attending college these days, schools must fight for all the students they can get.

→ .... since not as many students are going to

school as there used to be.

3 By increasing the school's academic rank, the school will attract both more students and better ones.

→ Good students will be more interested in ....

4 Unfortunately, many states are cutting general funding to schools, meaning that the schools must compensate for these lost funds in other ways.

→ Because ...., the schools need to

....

5 While not necessarily a glamorous job, the general management of the university is crucial to the wellbeing of the school.

→ The department that ...., but without it, the

school would ....

Summary

Even though students at universities are not pleased about ....,
the schools have some good reasons for doing so. First, they have to improve themselves
academically to ...., especially since fewer students
are going to college nowadays. This requires money. So does raising the school's
...., which will, in turn, attract better students to the school. A
lot of schools also receive funding from .... However, they are
receiving less funding nowadays. Finally, ... at these schools
need enough money to run properly, or else the school will suffer. The schools therefore need to
raise tuition to get more money.

B The following pairs of sentences are based on the listening. Complete each paraphrase by filling in the blanks with appropriate words or phrases. Then, complete the following summary.

1 Running a college is getting to be too expensive, but there are a few ways to offset this without raising students' fees.

→ Even though maintaining a school _____, schools
can still manage _____.

2 Professors and students should be looking at ourselves to improve our school.

→ The members of the school body, including _____,
should be able to _____.

3 Students performing better would help increase our school's ranking without us spending much money or raising tuition.

→ An inexpensive way to _____.

4 The universities will get free state-of-the-art facilities, which both students and faculty will be able to use.

→ The schools will be able to _____ that can be
accessed by _____.

5 And the corporations will know the students got an excellent education because they helped contribute to it.

→ Since the companies _____, they will
_____.

✍ Summary

It actually is possible for universities to increase _____ that they
offer without having to raise students' tuition. First, both _____
can improve themselves. The faculty can teach and prepare for classes better, and the
students can improve their performance as well. These actions should increase the school's
_____ without a need for a tuition hike. Schools should
also strike agreements with corporations. The corporations can provide the schools with
_____. The schools will, in turn, will produce well-educated
students that the companies will then be able to _____. This will
also help schools avoid raising the cost of tuition.

Synthesizing The following sentences are some important points from both the reading and the listening. Combine each pair of sentences to create your own sentence by using the given pattern.

1

Reading One ideal way to attract students is to ensure that the school provides them with an outstanding education.

Listening Professors could augment the quality of their lectures as well as develop better curriculums.

Combine The reading passage mentions that ....

.... ,

so the professor responds by claiming that ....

....

2

Reading Additionally, by increasing the school's academic rank, the school will attract both more students and better ones.

Listening And you, the students, could perform better both at school and after graduation.

Combine The writer claims that ....

.... ,

which leads the professor to declare that ....

....

3

Reading Unfortunately, many states are cutting general funding to schools, meaning that the schools must compensate for these lost funds in other ways.

Listening We should seek close ties with corporations.

Combine In response to the reading passage author's claim that ....

.... ,

the professor responds by saying that ....

....

4

Reading Most particularly hard hit are the funds for the general management of the university.

Listening First, we'll get free state-of-the-art facilities, which both students and faculty will be able to use.

Combine The writer claims that ....

.... ,

so the professor states that ....

....

Organization Review the notes from the reading and the listening. Complete the following chart with complete sentences.

Introduction	1 The professor states that .... 2 He then .... as to how they can do this.
Body 1	3 First, responding to the claim that .... , the professor claims that .... 4 He also mentions that .... 5 They can study harder and .... 6 With a higher academic rating, the school will ....
Body 2	7 In addition, since schools are seeing .... , the professor urges .... 8 He claims .... 9 These facilities will .... 10 The companies will also ....
Conclusion (Optional)	11 If a school follows the professor's suggestions, ...

Reading

Nowadays, many universities are raising their students' tuition. In some cases, the raises are quite substantial. While many students are not pleased with these increases, there are some legitimate reasons for the hikes.

First, universities are constantly striving to upgrade their educational quality. Since fewer people are attending college these days, schools must fight for all the students they can get. One ideal way to attract students is to ensure that the school provides them with an outstanding education. Additionally, by increasing the school's academic rank, the school will attract both more students and better ones. Since it costs money to enhance the quality of education, the school's budget must increase. Therefore, tuition must also go up.

Second, many universities are finding themselves short of cash these days. This is particularly true of state universities, which often depend upon the state government for the majority of their budgets. Unfortunately, many states are cutting general funding to schools. Most particularly hard hit are the funds for the general management of the university. While not necessarily a glamorous job, it is crucial to the wellbeing of the school. Without sufficient general management funds, many schools would be facing serious problems, so they need to compensate for the lost funds in other ways. It is therefore obvious why schools are increasing tuition every year.

Listening

Note Taking

01-08

Q Summarize the points made in the lecture, being sure to specifically explain how they answer the problems raised in the reading passage.

Exercise Read, listen, and answer the question following each step.

Reading Read the following passage and take notes.

Invasive species cause most of the worst problems in local ecosystems. The presence of a new species, particularly one at the top of the food chain, can destroy an ecosystem and cause numerous species to become extinct. One species that is causing numerous problems in America's waterways is the aquatic zebra mussel.

Native to Russia, the zebra mussel has invaded the Great Lakes and many other American lakes and rivers. The mussels attach themselves to the bottoms of boats, a convenient method that lets them travel easily. They also sometimes attach themselves to water pipes. This action results in clogged pipes, some of which are used to bring drinking water to cities. The blocked pipes cost the cities huge amounts of money to unblock. Zebra mussels also reproduce so rapidly that they often smother the spawning grounds of various fish and other mussels, thereby prohibiting their growth.

Secondly, zebra mussels in North America have very few natural enemies, meaning that it is difficult to eliminate them once they are established in a river or lake. Likewise, scientists have yet to discover an environmentally safe way to kill the zebra mussels. These two facts help contribute to the extremely rapid expansion of the zebra mussel. Should this expansion not be stopped, zebra mussels will soon be causing problems in virtually all of the country's waterways.

🔍 Words & Phrases

invasive (adj) aggressive; hostile
extinct (adj) nonexistent; vanished
aquatic (adj) of or relating to water
clog (v) to block
unblock (v) to clear out

smother (v) to suffocate; to cover entirely
spawning ground (n) a place where a species reproduces
prohibit (v) to ban; to stop
eliminate (v) to remove; to get rid of
virtually (adv) almost; nearly

✎ Note Taking

Invasive Zebra Mussels

1   Have left Russia and invaded waterways in United States
   - 1) _____ → costs lots of money to unblock
   - 2) _____ → smother spawning grounds of other species

2   Are difficult to remove
   - Have few 3) _____
   - No 4) _____ to kill them → expand rapidly

Listening

Listen to a lecture on the topic you just read about and take notes.

Note Taking

How to Get Rid of Zebra Mussels

01-09

1 Decontaminate ships better

- 1) ______________ with seawater → kills mussels
- Check the entire ship b/c mussels can 2) ______________

2 Use predators to kill zebra mussels

- Some 3) ______________ eat them → will get rid of mussels
- Researchers need to increase predators' numbers → will start to 4) ______________

Words & Phrases

estimate v to guess
mitigate v to ease; to lessen
procedure n a method; a way
implement v to utilize; to put into use
hitchhike v to ride along for free
sterilize v to purify; to disinfect; to sanitize
decontaminate v to clean; to purify
predator n a hunter
have an impact on phr to have an effect on
make a dent in phr to reduce

Comparing the Points

Complete the main points from both notes as complete sentences.

Zebra Mussels

Reading (Problems)	**Listening** (Solutions)
Zebra mussels have ______________, where they clog water pipes and ______________ of various fish and other mussels.	Before entering a waterway, ships' crews should ______________ with salt water, and they must ______________ since mussels can survive out of water for days.
The zebra mussels have few ______________, and there are no ______________ to kill them, so scientists have not been able to reduce their numbers.	There are ______________ that eat the mussels, so scientists must introduce them to the area and get their numbers to grow quickly so that they can ______________.

Paraphrasing & Summarizing

A The following pairs of sentences are based on the reading. Complete each paraphrase by filling in the blanks with appropriate words or phrases. Then, complete the following summary.

1 The presence of a new species, particularly one at the top of the food chain, can destroy an ecosystem and cause numerous species to become extinct.

→ When a top predator appears in a new environment, ...

2 Native to Russia, the zebra mussel has recently invaded the Great Lakes and many other American lakes and rivers.

→ While it comes from Russia, the zebra mussel ....

3 Zebra mussels also reproduce so rapidly that they often smother the spawning grounds of various fish and other mussels, thereby prohibiting their growth.

→ Since zebra mussels .... , they can

.... , which keeps these species from growing

larger in number.

4 Zebra mussels in North America have very few natural enemies, meaning that it is difficult to eliminate them once they are established in a river or lake.

→ In North America, the zebra mussel .... , which

makes it difficult to ....

5 Should this expansion not be stopped, zebra mussels will soon be causing problems in virtually all of the country's waterways.

→ If zebra mussels continue to expand their territories, ...

✍ Summary

When an invasive species moves into a new environment, it often causes problems for some native species, even causing them to .... This is the case for the zebra mussel. Coming from Russia, the mussel rode on boats to get to America. There, it .... , which are expensive to unblock. It also reproduces so rapidly that it covers up .... of other species, making these species reproduce more slowly. It is difficult to remove the mussels because they have few .... in North America. In addition, there is no .... to kill them. If the mussels are not killed, they will soon expand to all of America's waterways.

B The following pairs of sentences are based on the listening. Complete each paraphrase by filling in the blanks with appropriate words or phrases. Then, complete the following summary.

1 While the zebra mussel is causing problems, there are a couple of methods that could help mitigate the damage it's causing.

→ There are some ways to _____.

2 Before a boat enters a lake or river system, the ship's ballast should be sterilized with seawater, which kills the mussels.

→ The crew needs to _____.

3 Zebra mussels can survive out of water for several days, so the anchor chains and other parts out of water need to be decontaminated as well.

→ Zebra mussels do not always live in the water, so crews need to _____
_____.

4 There are some species of birds and fish that eat zebra mussels.

→ _____.

5 Researchers must discover a way quickly to increase the numbers of these species in the hope that they will start to make a dent in the number of mussels.

→ If scientists can _____, these animals will be able to
_____.

✐ **Summary**

While the zebra mussel has caused extremely expensive amounts of damage to
_____, there are some ways to control their numbers.
First, crew members on ships can do a couple of things. They can fill the ship's ballast
_____ since that will kill them. They should also check the entire
ship for mussels because they can _____ for a few days. In
addition, there are _____ that prey upon the zebra mussels. These
should be introduced to the waterways. Finally, since there are not enough of these predators,
people need to make sure they _____. These solutions can then
reduce the number of zebra mussels.

The following sentences are some important points from both the reading and the listening. Combine each pair of sentences to create your own sentence by using the given pattern.

1 **Reading** The mussels attach themselves to the bottoms of boats, a convenient method that lets them travel easily.

Listening Before a boat enters a lake or river system, the ship's ballast should be sterilized with seawater, which kills the mussels.

Combine The reading passage author writes that ....

.... ,

so the professor responds by arguing that ....

....

2 **Reading** Zebra mussels also reproduce so rapidly that they often smother the spawning grounds of various fish and other mussels, thereby prohibiting their growth.

Listening Zebra mussels can survive out of water for several days, so the anchor chains and other parts out of water need to be decontaminated as well.

Combine According to the professor, ...

.... ,

so that the mussels will not ....

.... , just like the reading passage describes.

3 **Reading** Secondly, zebra mussels in North America have very few natural enemies, meaning that it is difficult to eliminate them once they are established in a river or lake.

Listening The natural predators of the zebra mussel should be introduced to the waterways.

Combine As a response to the reading passage claim that ....

.... ,

the professor mentions that ....

....

4 **Reading** Likewise, scientists have yet to discover an environmentally safe way to kill the zebra mussels.

Listening Researchers must discover a way quickly to increase the numbers of these natural predators in the hope that they will start to make a dent in the number of mussels.

Combine Because ....

.... ,

the professor declares that ....

....

Review the notes from the reading and the listening. Complete the following chart with complete sentences.

Introduction	1 The professor talks about different ways to ....
	2 This is an invasive species from Russia that ....
	3 The professor provides ....
Body 1	4 First, she notes that ....
	5 She mentions this because ....
	6 The professor also notes that ....
	7 This will keep the mussels from ....
Body 2	8 Second, the professor states that ....
	9 While the reading claims that .... , the professor argues that ....
	10 She also thinks ....
	11 This will be beneficial because ....
Conclusion (Optional)	12 Although the zebra mussel is causing many problems, the professor seems confident that ....

Reading

Invasive species cause most of the worst problems in local ecosystems. The presence of a new species, particularly one at the top of the food chain, can destroy an ecosystem and cause numerous species to become extinct. One species that is causing numerous problems in America's waterways is the aquatic zebra mussel.

Native to Russia, the zebra mussel has recently invaded the Great Lakes and many other American lakes and rivers. The mussels attach themselves to the bottoms of boats, a convenient method that lets them travel easily. They also often attach themselves to water pipes. This action results in clogged pipes, some of which are used to bring drinking water to cities. The blocked pipes cost the cities huge amounts of money to unblock. Zebra mussels also reproduce so rapidly that they often smother the spawning grounds of various fish and other mussels, thereby prohibiting their growth.

Secondly, zebra mussels in North America have very few natural enemies, meaning that it is difficult to eliminate them once they are established in a river or lake. Likewise, scientists have yet to discover an environmentally safe way to kill the zebra mussels. These two facts help contribute to the extremely rapid expansion of the zebra mussel. Should this expansion not be stopped, zebra mussels will soon be causing problems in virtually all of the country's waterways.

Listening

Note Taking

01-09

Q Summarize the points made in the lecture, being sure to specifically explain how they answer the problems raised in the reading passage.

PART II

Writing for the Academic Discussion Task

In the academic discussion task, you will first be presented with a question by a professor that is written on a university online discussion board. You will then read two short responses by students in the class. These responses typically take opposite or different positions. Then, you must write your own response to the question posed by the professor. You will have 10 minutes to write an essay in response to the question. A typical essay is at least 100 words long.

Writing for an Academic Discussion Task

Overview

The second part of the Writing section of the TOEFL iBT is the TOEFL Writing for an Academic Discussion Task. This is a new task as of July 2023. You will see a question written by a university professor and then two responses by students. Your task is to write a response to the question. A typical response will be at least 100 words. You have ten minutes to write your response.

Question Types

1 Yes/No

Sometimes the professor asks a question and then requests that the students provide a yes-no answer. The professor may also ask the students if they agree or disagree with a statement. You should determine whether your answer to the question is yes or no or if you agree or disagree with the statement and then support your position with appropriate reasons and examples.

2 Preference

For these questions, the professor provides the students with a choice and asks them which of the two they prefer. You should determine which choice you prefer and then support your position with appropriate reasons and examples.

3 Open-Ended

The professor states a question that has no right or wrong answer but merely asks the students what they think about a topic. You should state your opinion regarding the question and then support your position with appropriate reasons and examples.

Useful Tips

1 The questions asked in this section come from a variety of topics. Many of the topics concern the environment and economics. But there are also questions based on sociology, political science, and other subjects in the liberal arts.

2 You do not require any specialized background knowledge to answer the professor's question. Simply read the question and the two students' responses, and then you can formulate your own answer.

3 Be sure to comment on the responses by both students.

4 Be sure to provide your own opinion. One way to do this is to add extra information to a comment made by one of the students.

5 The minimum response is 100 words, but you should try to write more than that.

6 There is no right or wrong answer. Simply defend your choice with good arguments and examples.

7 Try to write at least one complex sentence—a sentence with a conjunction such as *because, however, although,* or *since*—and two compound sentences—a sentence with a conjunction such as *and, but, or*, or *so* in your response. This will improve the quality of your writing and give you a chance to have a higher score.

Key Strategies

1 Brainstorming

▶ Read the professor's questions carefully to make sure that you understand it.

▶ Read each student's response to make sure that you understand their arguments.

▶ Brainstorm some ideas on scratch paper before you begin writing.

2 Outlining & Organizing

▶ Organize your response in outline form.

▶ Develop your ideas into complete sentences.

▶ Be sure to include an introductory statement as well as a conclusion.

3 Completing the Essay

▶ Make sure that your introductory statement is clear.

▶ Be sure to refer to the argument that each student makes.

▶ Provide clear reasons and examples.

▶ Write a concluding sentence.

▶ There is no need to write multiple paragraphs. Your entire response can be a single paragraph.

4 Writing & Checking Your Essay

▶ Read the professor's question and two student responses and plan your essay in 2 minutes.

▶ Spend 5-6 minutes writing your essay.

▶ Take 2-3 minutes to read over your essay to make changes and to find mistakes.

▶ Make sure you use proper grammar, have correct spelling, and write logical sentences.

Your professor is teaching a class on the history of science. Write a post responding to the professor's question.

In your response you should:

- express and support your opinion
- make a contribution to the discussion

An effective response will contain at least 100 words. You will have 10 minutes to write it.

Professor Wilkins

We live during a time when incredible scientific advances are constantly being made. Many of these discoveries are in the fields of medicine, chemistry, and biology. As a result, they can aid countless humans. Do you think important scientific discoveries should be shared for the benefit of humanity? Or should people and governments be allowed to keep them secret? Why?

Travis

The good of humanity must take precedence over everything else. When important scientific discoveries are made, they should be shared with the entire world. Imagine all of the medicines that have been created but not brought to market yet. Those pharmaceuticals could save millions of lives. We owe it to others to share discoveries to help them.

Sophia

Individuals and groups that make discoveries have no responsibility to share their discoveries with others. These people worked hard—often for years—and made discoveries that nobody else did. They should be allowed to monetize their discoveries and to try to make a profit. I see nothing wrong with people trying to benefit from their labors.

Sample Response

`Introductory sentence` While Travis makes some good points, I have the same opinion as Sophia. `Supporting Details 1` People who make discoveries are under no obligation to share them. As Sophia writes, the people who made the discoveries worked hard and did something nobody else could. They should get to profit from their discoveries. `Supporting Details 2` I would like to add that making a scientific discovery frequently costs enormous sums of money. The discoverers need to make their money back. If they share their secret with others, that will be impossible. `Conclusion` Forcing people to share what they learned will result in fewer people attempting to make discoveries since the profit motive will be gone.

Exercise 1 Follow the directions in each step.

Brainstorming & Outlining

A Read the professor's comment and brainstorm some ideas. Then, use the outline to generate your ideas.

Professor Cartwright

During our next class, we will be discussing online learning. It has had a highly disruptive effect on learning everywhere. That includes both at colleges and at other educational institutions. Here is something I would like everybody to think about on the discussion board. In your opinion, what is the most important result of online learning?

Words & Phrases

highly adv very; extremely
disruptive adj tending to cause an interruption to something
institution n an organization

opinion n a view, thought, or judgment about something
result n an effect; something that happens as a consequence

✦ **Outline for Brainstorming**

The Most Important Result of Online Learning

Make Education Available to All		Cheaper than Physical Schools	
Reason 1 No need to attend physical school	**Reason 2** Can remain in hometown → still study	**Reason 1** Financial status = not important	**Reason 2** Not prevented from attending college due to no money

B Read the following comments by two students and complete the summary notes.

Jacqueline

In my mind, making education available to everyone in the world is the most important result of online learning. Thanks to the Internet, people no longer need to attend a physical school to be educated. Instead, they can utilize online learning from their homes—or anywhere else, for that matter—and still receive a quality education.

📖 **Words & Phrases**

available adj ready for use; accessible
attend v to go to a class, school, etc.
physical adj having a material existence

utilize v to use
quality adj being of high level

✏️ **Summary Notes: Jacqueline**

Make Education Available to All

1   No need to [1] ....

2   Can be educated [2] ....
    • Can study [3] ....
    • Can still get [4] ....

Harold

Most online classes are much cheaper than comparable classes at a college or university. As a result, an individual's financial status has no bearing on that person's ability to learn more. Lots of people cannot attend college due to the high price of tuition. That is no longer the case thanks to inexpensive online classes.

📖 **Words & Phrases**

comparable adj like; similar
financial adj relating to money
status n a condition or state

bearing n a relation; a connection
tuition n money paid for school, a class, etc.

✏️ **Summary Notes: Harold**

Cheaper than Physical Schools

1   [1] .... = no bearing on ability to [2] ....

2   Many people = [3] .... because of high [4] ....
    • Inexpensive [5] .... = no longer the case

Review the outline and the summary notes on the previous pages and then complete each chart.

● Supporting Jacqueline's Opinion

Introduction	1 I like the answers that ...., but ....
Body 1	2 For me, ... 3 Most online classes .... 4 They can therefore ....
Body 2	5 The only important thing is that .... 6 This benefits .... 7 For instance, ..., yet ....
Conclusion	8 This enables them to ....

● Supporting Harold's Opinion

Introduction	1 The fact that ....
Body 1	2 Not everyone is .... 3 They ...., or perhaps .... 4 Whatever the case, ...
Body 2	5 This feature is also .... 6 They .... 7 But as long as ...., they can ....
Conclusion	8 To me, ...

Follow the directions and write a response. You can refer to the outline and the summary notes.

 Your professor is teaching a class on education. Write a post responding to the professor's question.

In your response you should:

- express and support your opinion
- make a contribution to the discussion

An effective response will contain at least 100 words. You will have 10 minutes to write it.

Professor
Ward

Smartphones are one of the most influential technologies of the past few decades. They have numerous functions aside from being able to make telephone calls and send text messages. However, they can also be distracting to people, particularly teens. Do you believe that high schools should ban students from bringing smartphones to school? Why or why not?

📖 **Words & Phrases**

influential [adj] having the power to have an effect on something
technology [n] the application of knowledge in a certain field
function [n] a use; a purpose

distracting [adj] causing a person's attention to be drawn to something different
teen [n] a teenager; a person between thirteen and nineteen years of age

✦ Outline for Brainstorming

Banning Smartphones from High School

Should Be Banned	Should Not Be Banned
Reason Students play with phones	**Reason** Can be used as research tools
Example Ignore teachers → neglect studies	**Example** Can help with assignments

Carter

High schools should definitely prohibit students from bringing smartphones to school. So many students ignore their teachers in favor of playing with their phones during class. As a result, they neglect their studies, which hinders their education and harms their future prospects. High school students have no reason at all to bring smartphones to school.

Beatrice

I think it is acceptable for high school students to bring their smartphones to school. Of course, they should be barred from touching their phones during class to avoid distractions. After all, smartphones can be employed as research tools since they can access the Internet. Students can therefore take advantage of this ability and use them to learn.

🔍 Words & Phrases

prohibit Ⓥ to ban; not to allow

ignore Ⓥ to refuse to notice; not to pay attention on purpose

neglect Ⓥ to give little attention to; to disregard

hinder Ⓥ to hold back; to prevent

prospect Ⓝ a chance; a possibility; something expected in the future

acceptable ⓐⓓⓙ good enough; permissible; allowed

bar Ⓥ to prevent; to stop

employ Ⓥ to use

tool Ⓝ a handheld device that does some kind of work

take advantage of ⓟⓗⓡ to use to one's benefit

✏️ Summary Notes

Carter
1 1) ....
• Play w/phones in class
2 Neglect studies
• 2) ....
• Harms future prospects

Beatrice
1 Acceptable to bring to school
• Barred from touching phones during class
• 1) ....
2 Employed as research tools
• 2) ....
• Use smartphones to learn

_____

_____

_____

_____

_____

_____

_____

_____

_____

_____

_____

_____

_____

_____

_____

Self-Evaluation   Check your response by answering the following questions.

	Yes	No
1 Did you address the professor's question?	☐	☐
2 Did you refer to the comments by the two students?	☐	☐
3 Did you express your own opinion?	☐	☐
4 Did you provide examples to support your opinion?	☐	☐
5 Did you organize your response well?	☐	☐
6 Did you use correct grammar?	☐	☐
7 Did you use correct punctuation?	☐	☐
8 Did you spell all of the words correctly?	☐	☐

Unit 10　Sociology I

Exercise 1 Follow the directions in each step.

Brainstorming & Outlining

A Read the professor's comment and brainstorm some ideas. Then, use the outline to generate your ideas.

Urban centers worldwide are increasing in population nowadays. One result is that these cities must constantly deal with traffic problems. These include crowded roads and traffic jams that can last for hours. What do you think the best way for cities to solve their traffic problems is? Why do you feel that way?

Words & Phrases

urban adj relating to a city
population n the number of people living in a certain area
deal with phr to handle; to manage

crowded adj full of something, especially people
traffic jam n a situation in which there are many slowly moving vehicles on a road

✦ **Outline for Brainstorming**

The Best Way to Solve Traffic Problems

Emphasize Public Transportation		Widen Roads	
Reason 1 Expand bus and subway systems	**Reason 2** Will reduce traffic on roads	**Reason 1** More vehicles on roads	**Reason 2** Let commuters get to destinations faster

B Read the following comments by two students and complete the summary notes.

Madeline

Clearly, the best way to handle traffic problems is to emphasize public transportation. Cities should build up and expand bus and subway systems. If the buses and the subways extend to enough places, including nearby suburbs, more people will quit driving. This will alleviate traffic jams and reduce congestion on roads.

Words & Phrases

handle [v] to take care of
emphasize [v] to stress
suburb [n] a small city located near a bigger one

alleviate [v] to ease; to make less
congestion [n] the act of being clogged or stopped

Summary Notes: Madeline

Emphasize Public Transportation

1   Build up [1]) ....
    • Expand them into [2]) ....

2   More people will [3]) ....
    • Alleviate [4]) ....
    • Reduce [5]) .... on roads

Leonard

In my opinion, cities ought to widen many of the roads, especially elevated ones which numerous vehicles ride on. By making these roads broader, there will be more space for cars, trucks, and other vehicles. This will help eliminate traffic jams and let commuters get to work and home much faster than normal.

Words & Phrases

widen [v] to increase the width, length, or extent of
elevated [adj] being above the ground or in the air
eliminate [v] to get rid of

commuter [n] a person who travels from home to work or school and back

Summary Notes: Leonard

Widen Roads

1   Widen [1]) ....
    • Especially [2]) .... → numerous vehicles ride on

2   Will be [3]) .... for cars, trucks, and other vehicles
    • Help [4]) ....
    • Let commuters get to [5]) .... faster

Review the outline and the summary notes on the previous pages and then complete each chart.

● **Supporting New Ideas: Banning Vehicles from Roads**

Introduction	**1** Madeline and Leonard .... , but I ....
Body 1	**2** I suggest that .... **3** For instance, ... **4** This would ....
Body 2	**5** This .... **6** It .... **7** Another benefit would be that .... , so ....
Conclusion	**8** My solution ....

● **Supporting New Ideas: Carpooling in Cities**

Introduction	**1** I like .... , but I ....
Body 1	**2** A simple way to .... **3** Many cars .... **4** If people .... **5** Those people's cars ....
Body 2	**6** Drivers would also .... **7** They could ....
Conclusion	**8** This simple solution could ....

Exercise 2 Follow the directions and write a response. You can refer to the outline and the summary notes.

Q Your professor is teaching a class on sociology. Write a post responding to the professor's question.

In your response you should:

- express and support your opinion
- make a contribution to the discussion

An effective response will contain at least 100 words. You will have 10 minutes to write it.

Professor
Robinson

Many families formerly had three, four, or more children. Recently, the number of children per family has declined though. Among the reasons are financial worries and concerns about overpopulation. However, for a country's population to remain stable, the fertility rate must be around two. Do you believe families should have two or more children or one or no children? Why?

Words & Phrases

formerly adv previously
decline v to go down
overpopulation n the condition of having too many people living in a certain area

stable adj steady; constant
fertility rate n the average number of children born to a woman in her lifetime

✦ Outline for Brainstorming

The Number of Children in a Family

Two or More	One or None
Reason World is not overpopulated	**Reason** World has too many problems
Example Many uninhabited places → can build cities for people in them	**Example** Children likely to suffer

Tyler

Children are awesome, so I wish families would have multiple children. The world is actually not overpopulated as there are enormous uninhabited tracts of land that humans could move to. Children are also the future, so humanity needs as many children as possible to ensure that the human race does not go extinct.

Amanda

People should stop being so selfish by having lots of kids. Having one child or none should be the objective for married couples. The world has so many problems, including hunger, wars, and environmental issues. We should not be bringing more children into a world in which they are likely to suffer and have miserable lives.

🔍 Words & Phrases

awesome adj amazing; wonderful
multiple adj many
uninhabited adj not occupied or lived in by people
tract n an area of land
humanity n the human race as a whole
selfish adj concerned only with oneself

objective n a goal
hunger n a condition in which a person is weak from a lack of food
suffer v to undergo or experience something negative or harmful
miserable adj awful; terrible; very bad

✍ Summary Notes

Tyler
1 World = not overpopulated
• Enormous uninhabited tracts of land
• 1) _____
2 Children = future of humanity
• 2) _____
• Can ensure humans don't go extinct

Amanda
1 Selfish to have lots of kids
• 1 or 0 children = objective for married couples
2 World has many problems
• 1) _____
• 2) _____

_____

_____

_____

_____

_____

_____

_____

_____

_____

_____

_____

_____

_____

_____

_____

_____

Self-Evaluation Check your response by answering the following questions.

	Yes	No
1 Did you address the professor's question?	☐	☐
2 Did you refer to the comments by the two students?	☐	☐
3 Did you express your own opinion?	☐	☐
4 Did you provide examples to support your opinion?	☐	☐
5 Did you organize your response well?	☐	☐
6 Did you use correct grammar?	☐	☐
7 Did you use correct punctuation?	☐	☐
8 Did you spell all of the words correctly?	☐	☐

Exercise 1 Follow the directions in each step.

Brainstorming & Outlining

A Read the professor's comment and brainstorm some ideas. Then, use the outline to generate your ideas.

Professor
Olsen

We will be discussing small businesses in our next class. Here is something I want you to post about on the discussion board. Many people going into business seek a partner. In your opinion, what is the most important criterion when choosing a potential business partner? Why do you believe that?

Words & Phrases

seek v to look for; to search for
partner n a person with whom another does something
opinion n a thought; a belief

criterion n a standard on which a person makes a judgment
potential adj relating to possibility

✦ **Outline for Brainstorming**

> **The Most Important Criterion for a Business Partner**

Strong Work Ethic		Creativity	
Reason 1	**Reason 2**	**Reason 1**	**Reason 2**
Both partners work hard → business will succeed	Only one works hard → friction	Need to make business different from others	Attract attention from customers and investors

B Read the following comments by two students and complete the summary notes.

Diana

A strong work ethic is vital in a business partner. If both partners work hard, the venture is likely to succeed. If one partner has a poor work ethic, the business could fail. In addition, it could cause friction between the two partners since one will be working harder than the other.

📖 **Words & Phrases**

work ethic [n] a determination to work hard; a set of values based on working hard
vital [adj] important; crucial

venture [n] an undertaking, especially related to business
fail [v] not to succeed; to do very poorly or badly
friction [n] disagreement; a clash between people with different views

✏️ **Summary Notes: Diana**

Strong Work Ethic

1   1) .... to have
     • Both work 2) .... = venture likely to 3) ....
     • 4) .... work ethic = venture could 5) ....

2   6) .... between partners
     • One works 7) .... than other

Bruce

Creativity is what I would look for. There are so many similar businesses these days. A creative partner would be able to make the new business different from the others. This would attract attention from customers and investors and would therefore increase the likelihood of the business making a profit.

📖 **Words & Phrases**

creativity [n] the ability to make or imagine new things
attention [n] notice; observation
investor [n] a person who commits money to a project in an attempt to make a positive return

likelihood [n] the chance that something will happen; a probability
profit [n] money that one makes from a job

✏️ **Summary Notes: Bruce**

Creativity

1   Many 1) ....
     • Creative partner makes business 2) ....

2   Attract attention from 3) ....
     • Increase likelihood of making profit

Organization Review the outline and the summary notes on the previous pages and then complete each chart.

● **Supporting New Ideas: Having Business Experience**

Introduction	1 While Diana and Bruce _____, I believe _____.
Body 1	2 For me, _____. 3 Many people _____; however, _____. 4 This results in _____.
Body 2	5 A partner _____. 6 For example, _____. 7 The person would also _____.
Conclusion	8 To me, _____.

● **Supporting New Ideas: Being Honest**

Introduction	1 I like _____, yet _____.
Body 1	2 In my view, honesty _____. 3 An honest person _____. 4 I have read about _____. 5 That _____.
Body 2	6 In addition, _____ _____. 7 That will _____.
Conclusion	8 As a result, _____.

Follow the directions and write a response. You can refer to the outline and the summary notes.

 Q Your professor is teaching a class on economics. Write a post responding to the professor's question.

In your response you should:

- express and support your opinion
- make a contribution to the discussion

An effective response will contain at least 100 words. You will have 10 minutes to write it.

Professor
Kimble

Advertisers these days are highly sophisticated. They normally target their advertisements toward the people who are most likely to purchase their goods or services. However, some targeted ads are aimed at children. Some people believe these ads manipulate children into buying unnecessary products. Do you think targeted ads for children should be prohibited? Why or why not?

Words & Phrases

sophisticated adj complex; refined
target v to make a goal or objective of
aim v to point; to direct toward a certain objective

manipulate v to control, often through unfair or clever means; to take advantage of
prohibit v to ban; not to allow

✦ Outline for Brainstorming

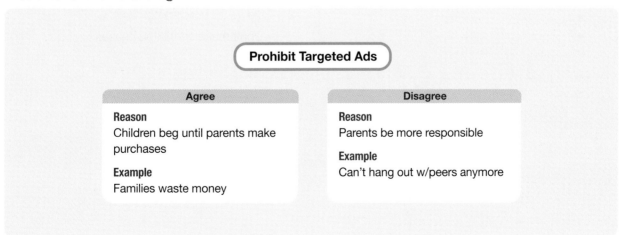

Prohibit Targeted Ads

Agree	Disagree
Reason Children beg until parents make purchases	**Reason** Parents be more responsible
Example Families waste money	**Example** Can't hang out w/peers anymore

Julie

It is wrong for advertisers to target children, so I believe these ads should be banned. Children usually have little or no money to spend themselves. Still, they can beg and plead until their parents make purchases. The result is that families waste their money on items they do not really need.

Robert

I see no problem with advertisers targeting children, even very young ones. Parents merely need to be responsible and should monitor their children's TV viewing. Plus, parents can just tell their children no and not make certain purchases. Parents must be strong and not give in to their children's desires.

Words & Phrases

ban v to disallow an activity; to prohibit
spend v to use, as in money
beg v to ask for, often in an urgent way
plead v to make an earnest appeal
waste v to spend money in a careless manner
responsible adj being the person who must answer for something

monitor v to watch, often closely
viewing n the act of watching
give in to phr to surrender; to agree to something after first saying no to it
desire n an urge; an impulse

Summary Notes

Julie

1 Wrong to target children
   • Should be banned

2 Children have little or no money
   • 1) _____
   • 2) _____

Robert

1 No problem targeting children
   • 1) _____
   • Monitor children's TV viewing

2 Parents tell children no
   • Don't make certain purchases
   • 2) _____

Self-Evaluation Check your response by answering the following questions.

	Yes	No
1 Did you address the professor's question?	☐	☐
2 Did you refer to the comments by the two students?	☐	☐
3 Did you express your own opinion?	☐	☐
4 Did you provide examples to support your opinion?	☐	☐
5 Did you organize your response well?	☐	☐
6 Did you use correct grammar?	☐	☐
7 Did you use correct punctuation?	☐	☐
8 Did you spell all of the words correctly?	☐	☐

Exercise 1   Follow the directions in each step.

Brainstorming & Outlining

A   Read the professor's comment and brainstorm some ideas. Then, use the outline to generate your ideas.

Professor
Thompson

These days, countless people own personal vehicles and travel in airplanes. However, these vehicles are also responsible for spewing harmful emissions into the atmosphere. This is causing air pollution and other problems. Consider this: People should be charged a fee whenever they travel by automobile or plane due to the pollution each creates. Do you agree or disagree? Why?

Words & Phrases

countless adj many; too many to be counted
spew v to expel; to shoot out
emission n something that is sent out

atmosphere n all of the air surrounding the Earth
pollution n the condition of being made dirty or unclean, often by humans

✦ Outline for Brainstorming

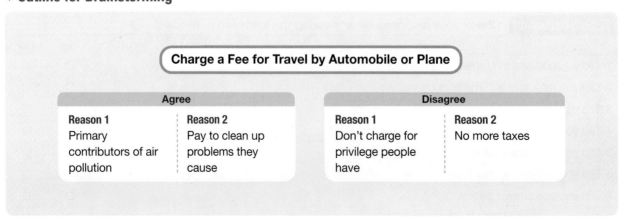

Charge a Fee for Travel by Automobile or Plane

Agree		Disagree	
Reason 1	**Reason 2**	**Reason 1**	**Reason 2**
Primary contributors of air pollution	Pay to clean up problems they cause	Don't charge for privilege people have	No more taxes

B Read the following comments by two students and complete the summary notes.

Orville

Air pollution has so many negative effects, and cars and planes are primary contributors of air pollution. I therefore agree with the statement. Charging a fee for driving and flying would provide funds that would allow countries to combat air pollution. People would thus be paying to clean up the problems they are causing. I find that fair.

📖 **Words & Phrases**

negative adj lacking positive characteristics or qualities
primary adj main
contributor n someone or something that gives or supplies something

fund n money that one has access to and can spend
combat v to fight

✍ **Summary Notes: Orville**

Agree
1 Air pollution has ¹⁾ ....
• Cars + planes = ²⁾ .... of ³⁾ ....
2 Fee provides ⁴⁾ .... to clean up air pollution
• People pay to clean up ⁵⁾ ....
• ⁶⁾ .... solution

Mae

I could not disagree more with this statement. Millions of people in this country have been driving and flying for decades. Suddenly charging a fee for that privilege is wrong. It would basically be a tax, and the government is already taxing the people enough. People have the right to travel and should not have to pay to do that.

📖 **Words & Phrases**

charge v to ask or demand a payment
privilege n a right
basically adv for the most part

tax v to impose a payment on people, mainly done by the government
right n something a person is entitled to do or has the power to do

✍ **Summary Notes: Mae**

Disagree
1 People driving and flying for ¹⁾ ....
• Wrong to ²⁾ .... for privilege
2 Fee would be ³⁾ ....
• ⁴⁾ .... people enough
• People have ⁵⁾ .... → shouldn't have to ⁶⁾ ....

Organization Review the outline and the summary notes on the previous pages and then complete each chart.

● Supporting Orville's Opinion

Introduction	1 While this topic _____ , I agree with Orville and _____ .
Body 1	2 Orville correctly notes that _____ . 3 Since _____ , it is logical to _____ .
Body 2	4 Something else is that _____ . 5 This would result in _____ , so _____ . 6 We must think about _____ . 7 We should _____ .
Conclusion	8 I therefore _____ .

● Supporting Mae's Opinion

Introduction	1 Although it is true that _____ , I do not agree _____ .
Body 1	2 As Mae remarks, _____ . 3 People should not _____ .
Body 2	4 Let me add that _____ . 5 For drivers, _____ . 6 Some people would _____ .
Conclusion	7 Although air pollution _____ , charging a driving and flying fee _____ .

Q Your professor is teaching a class on environmental science. Write a post responding to the professor's question.

In your response you should:

- express and support your opinion
- make a contribution to the discussion

An effective response will contain at least 100 words. You will have 10 minutes to write it.

Professor
Jackson

In our next class, we will talk about how humans are responsible for many species being endangered and going extinct. Here is a question for you to consider for the discussion board: Should humans take action to protect endangered species and to help them maintain or increase their numbers? Why or why not?

Words & Phrases

responsible (adj) liable as the primary cause of something

endangered (adj) being in small numbers and having the possibility of dying out

go extinct (phr) to die out; to cease to exist, often as a species

protect (v) to take care of; to keep safe

maintain (v) to keep in one's present state; to keep from declining or failing

---

✦ Outline for Brainstorming

Protecting Endangered Species

Support	Do Not Support
Reason Humans = stewards of the Earth	**Reason** Species always go extinct
Example Create nature preserves → protect animals there	**Example** Should let animals that don't adapt die out

Leia

It is a shame how we humans have made species like the dodo extinct and have reduced the numbers of species on every continent. We should definitely act to protect endangered species. A simple way would be to establish more nature preserves in which animals can live without fear of being hunted or harmed in any way.

Brandon

I do not believe we should act to protect endangered species. For one thing, there are uninhabited places around the world where animals live in peace with humans nowhere in sight. For another thing, species have gone extinct throughout the Earth's history. If a species is unable to adapt to conditions on the Earth, then we should let it die out.

🔍 Words & Phrases

shame n a situation that is sad or unfortunate

dodo n a flightless bird that went extinct hundreds of years ago

continent n one of the seven enormous landmasses on the Earth

establish v to create; to found; to make

nature preserve n a place with few people and where plants and animals are protected

peace n a state of quiet with a lack of violence

nowhere adv not in any place

history n a record of events from the past

adapt v to change to become fit for something; to become suitable

condition n a state of being

✏️ Summary Notes

Leia

1 Shame that humans make species go extinct
   • 1) _____

2 2) _____
   • Animals can live in them
   • No fear of being hunted or harmed

Brandon

1 Many uninhabited places around world
   • Animals live in peace
   • 1) _____

2 2) _____
   • Species unable to adapt = let it die out

_____

_____

_____

_____

_____

_____

_____

_____

_____

_____

_____

_____

_____

_____

_____

_____

Self-Evaluation Check your response by answering the following questions.

		Yes	No
1	Did you address the professor's question?	☐	☐
2	Did you refer to the comments by the two students?	☐	☐
3	Did you express your own opinion?	☐	☐
4	Did you provide examples to support your opinion?	☐	☐
5	Did you organize your response well?	☐	☐
6	Did you use correct grammar?	☐	☐
7	Did you use correct punctuation?	☐	☐
8	Did you spell all of the words correctly?	☐	☐

Exercise 1 Follow the directions in each step.

Brainstorming & Outlining

A Read the professor's comment and brainstorm some ideas. Then, use the outline to generate your ideas.

Professor
Jefferson

In our class tomorrow, we will cover various teaching methods. Here is something I want you to contemplate before class: Some professors instruct their classes primarily by lecturing during the entire period. Other professors require student participation in their lessons, typically by having class discussions at times. Which type of class do you prefer? Why?

🔍 **Words & Phrases**

cover v to discuss; to talk about
contemplate v to think about; to ponder
lecture v to teach

participation n the act of taking part in an activity
class discussion n a time when students contribute to a class by talking

✦ **Outline for Brainstorming**

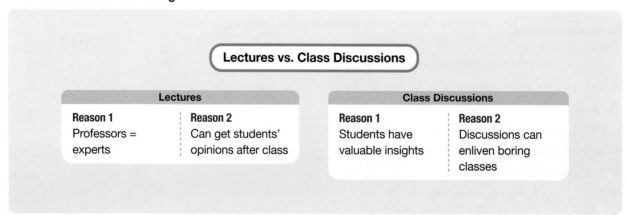

Lectures vs. Class Discussions

Lectures		Class Discussions	
Reason 1	**Reason 2**	**Reason 1**	**Reason 2**
Professors = experts	Can get students' opinions after class	Students have valuable insights	Discussions can enliven boring classes

B Read the following comments by two students and complete the summary notes.

Rudolph

Classes in which professors only lecture are my preference. Professors, after all, are experts in their fields, so I would prefer to get my money's worth by having the professor teach during the entire class. If I want to hear students' opinions, I can talk to my classmates as soon as class is dismissed.

Words & Phrases

preference (n) the act of choosing one thing over another
expert (n) a person with a great deal of knowledge of a topic
get one's money's worth (phr) to get in value what one pays for something

entire (adj) complete; total
dismiss (v) to let someone leave

Summary Notes: Rudolph

Lectures
1   Professors = 1) ....
• Want to get 2) ....
• Have professor teach 3) ....
2   Talk to students 4) .... if want their opinions

Angelina

I actually prefer classes in which there are discussions. Many students have valuable insights which they can provide to their classmates. I have learned a lot from previous class discussions and feel that I have contributions to make to them at times, too. Plus, discussions can enliven some classes, which can get boring if professors are just droning on.

Words & Phrases

insight (n) the ability to understand a situation
previous (adj) prior; happening in the past
contribution (n) something added to another thing

enliven (v) to make more interesting; to give life to
drone on (phr) to speak for a long time but not to say anything interesting

Summary Notes: Angelina

Class Discussions
1   Students have 1) ....
• Can provide 2) .... for classmates
• Have learned from 3) ....
• Have my 4) .... to make
2   Can 5) .... some classes
• Boring → professors 6) ....

Organization Review the outline and the summary notes on the previous pages and then complete each chart.

● Supporting Rudolph's Opinion

Introduction	1 This is an interesting question that ....
Body 1	2 Personally, I agree with Rudolph and .... 3 My major is ...., and I .... 4 Professors who ....
Body 2	5 Plus, I am not .... 6 Students frequently .... 7 So they do not ....
Conclusion	8 Overall, ...

● Supporting Angelina's Opinion

Introduction	1 Angelina has the right idea as ....
Body 1	2 As she notes, ... 3 This is particularly true in .... 4 Thanks to some discussions, I ....
Body 2	5 In addition, when ...., students can .... 6 This requires the professor to .... and to .... 7 Still, ...
Conclusion	8 For those two reasons, I ....

Exercise 2 Follow the directions and write a response. You can refer to the outline and the summary notes.

Your professor is teaching a class on education. Write a post responding to the professor's question.

In your response you should:

- express and support your opinion
- make a contribution to the discussion

An effective response will contain at least 100 words. You will have 10 minutes to write it.

Professor
Saville

Sometimes individuals or organizations make large donations to universities. Some of these financial gifts can be millions or even tens of millions of dollars. Universities must then decide how to spend the money. They could build new facilities or renovate others, hire more faculty, or do something else. In your opinion, how should universities spend large donations? Why?

📖 Words & Phrases

donation Ⓝ something, especially money, given to someone
gift Ⓝ a present

facility Ⓝ a building used for a specific purpose
renovate Ⓥ to restore to a better condition
faculty Ⓥ members of the teaching staff at a school

✦ Outline for Brainstorming

How to Spend Donation to University

More Scholarships	Hiring More Faculty Members
Reason Tuition too expensive	**Reason** Students can learn more
Example Financial need scholarships = highly welcomed	**Example** Can't hang out w/peers anymore

Francine

Providing more scholarships for students is how the university should spend the money. Tuition is so high nowadays that many students cannot afford it. Scholarships based on financial need would be highly welcomed. So would academic scholarships awarded to students with stellar grades. These students should be rewarded for being outstanding performers.

Anthony

Universities exist to teach students, and they can best fulfill this objective by hiring more faculty members. Increasing the number of professors would enable students to learn more information since the professors would have varied academic interests. Class sizes would also shrink, allowing students to get more face time with their instructors.

Words & Phrases

scholarship [n] a grant of money to a student
welcome [v] to appreciate; to approve of
academic [adj] relating to school, especially to learning
stellar [adj] outstanding
reward [v] to give money to a person in return for doing something

fulfill [v] to complete
enable [v] to let; to allow
varied [adj] being of different kinds
shrink [v] to become smaller in size, amount, or quantity
face time [n] time spent meeting someone face to face

Summary Notes

Francine
1 Provide more scholarships
• Tuition too high
• 1) ....
2 Need-based scholarships welcome
3 2) ....
• Reward students w/stellar grades
• Give to outstanding performers

Anthony
1 1) ....
• Students can learn more
• Professors have varied academic interests
2 2) ....
• Students get more face time w/instructors

Self-Evaluation Check your response by answering the following questions.

	Yes	No
1 Did you address the professor's question?	☐	☐
2 Did you refer to the comments by the two students?	☐	☐
3 Did you express your own opinion?	☐	☐
4 Did you provide examples to support your opinion?	☐	☐
5 Did you organize your response well?	☐	☐
6 Did you use correct grammar?	☐	☐
7 Did you use correct punctuation?	☐	☐
8 Did you spell all of the words correctly?	☐	☐

Exercise 1 Follow the directions in each step.

Brainstorming & Outlining

A Read the professor's comment and brainstorm some ideas. Then, use the outline to generate your ideas.

Professor
Garner

In next week's class, we will cover the changing nature of work. For example, white-collar employees traditionally worked in an office every day. However, thanks primarily to the Internet, it is now possible for people to work from home. Here is a question for you: Which would you prefer, to work in an office or to work from home? Why?

Words & Phrases

nature (n) a state or condition
white-collar employee (n) a salaried worker who often works in an office

traditionally (adv) typically; normally
thanks to (phr) because of; due to
primarily (adv) mainly

✦ Outline for Brainstorming

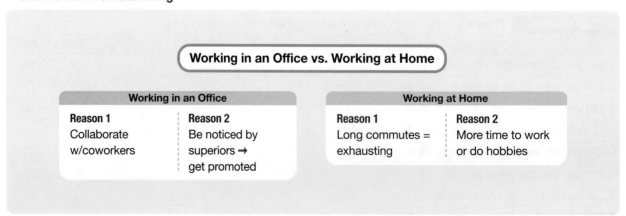

Working in an Office vs. Working at Home			
Working in an Office		**Working at Home**	
Reason 1	**Reason 2**	**Reason 1**	**Reason 2**
Collaborate w/coworkers	Be noticed by superiors → get promoted	Long commutes = exhausting	More time to work or do hobbies

B Read the following comments by two students and complete the summary notes.

Douglas

I understand the desire to work from home, but I would prefer to work in an office environment. I would enjoy collaborating on projects with coworkers. That would only be possible if I were working in an office. Additionally, working face to face is the best way to be noticed by superiors, which can lead to promotions.

📖 **Words & Phrases**

collaborate (v) to work together with another person on a project
coworker (n) a person who works at the same company or in the same department

face to face (phr) within sight of another person
superior (n) a manager; a supervisor
promotion (n) the act of being given a higher position

✒ **Summary Notes: Douglas**

Working in an Office
1 Enjoy [1] ....
• Only possible if [2] ....
2 Work [3] ....
• Get noticed by [4] ....
• Leads to [5] ....

Kate

I would love the opportunity to work from home. My parents both have long commutes to their jobs, and they come home exhausted after driving so long each day. By working at home, I could avoid commutes, which would save energy. That would also give me more time either to work or to pursue personal hobbies of mine.

📖 **Words & Phrases**

commute (n) the act of going from one's home to school or work and back
exhausted (adj) very tired
avoid (v) to keep from doing something

pursue (v) to engage or take part in
hobby (n) an activity a person does that is usually for relaxation

✒ **Summary Notes: Kate**

Working at Home
1 Parents have [1] ....
• Come home [2] .... from [3] ....
• [4] .... commutes ➜ save [5] ....
2 [6] .... for other activities
• Do more [7] ....
• Pursue [8] ....

Review the outline and the summary notes on the previous pages and then complete each chart.

● **Supporting Douglas's Opinion**

Introduction	1 I am in full agreement with Douglas that _____ .
Body 1	2 He is right that _____ . 3 I am _____ . 4 To do that, I must _____ . 5 That means _____ .
Body 2	6 Another advantage is _____ . 7 Networking _____ , which can _____ .
Conclusion	8 In my opinion, _____ .

● **Supporting Kate's Opinion**

Introduction	1 I understand how Douglas thinks, but _____ .
Body 1	2 Like Kate's parents, _____ . 3 However, _____ . 4 That has resulted in _____ . 5 I want _____ .
Body 2	6 Additionally, _____ , so _____ . 7 Being productive, I _____ . 8 That will _____ .
Conclusion	9 There are _____ .

Exercise 2 Follow the directions and write a response. You can refer to the outline and the summary notes.

 Q Your professor is teaching a class on the history of technology. Write a post responding to the professor's question.

In your response you should:

- express and support your opinion
- make a contribution to the discussion

An effective response will contain at least 100 words. You will have 10 minutes to write it.

Professor
Porter

We are going to discuss artificial intelligence (AI) in Friday's class. I am interested in knowing your thoughts on it ahead of time. AI is becoming more prevalent in society every year. As AI is developed further, do you believe it will have a beneficial or harmful effect on mankind? Why do you think so?

📖 **Words & Phrases**

artificial adj manmade; not natural
prevalent adj widespread; dominant
develop v to create or improve over time

beneficial adj producing good or positive results
mankind n the human race; all humans considered together

✦ **Outline for Brainstorming**

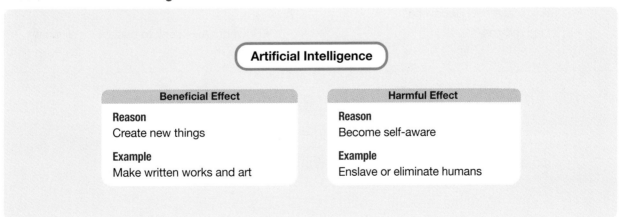

Artificial Intelligence

Beneficial Effect	Harmful Effect
Reason Create new things	**Reason** Become self-aware
Example Make written works and art	**Example** Enslave or eliminate humans

Yvette

I foresee AI having plenty of positive effects on humanity. For instance, there are already AI programs that help people create written works and art. These programs allow people to express their artistic abilities. AI is also being used to assist scientists as they strive to make new discoveries that will help millions of humans.

Noah

There are plenty of ways AIs could produce harmful or disastrous results. Today, AI is in its early stages, but there are still problems. Some AIs tasked to do academic reports create fake studies. In addition, as AI improves, so does the likelihood of it becoming self-aware. A powerful AI like that could seek to enslave or eliminate humanity.

📖 Words & Phrases

foresee v to see something before it happens

express v to show; to reflect

artistic adj relating to art or artists

scientist n a person who is knowledgeable about science

strive v to spend a lot of energy doing something; to try hard

disastrous adj terrible; harmful

task v to assign a job or duty to

fake adj not real or accurate; false

self-aware adj being aware of one's own personality

enslave v to make someone a slave

✏ Summary Notes

Yvette

1 AI programs help people
   - 1) _____
   - Let people express artistic abilities

2 2) _____
   - Strive to make new discoveries
   - Will help millions

Noah

1 Could produce harmful or disastrous results
   - In early stages
   - Still has problems
   - 1) _____

2 2) _____
   - Powerful AI ➡ seek to enslave or eliminate humanity

Self-Evaluation Check your response by answering the following questions.

	Yes	No
1 Did you address the professor's question?	☐	☐
2 Did you refer to the comments by the two students?	☐	☐
3 Did you express your own opinion?	☐	☐
4 Did you provide examples to support your opinion?	☐	☐
5 Did you organize your response well?	☐	☐
6 Did you use correct grammar?	☐	☐
7 Did you use correct punctuation?	☐	☐
8 Did you spell all of the words correctly?	☐	☐

Unit **15** Sociology II

Exercise 1 Follow the directions in each step.

Brainstorming & Outlining

A Read the professor's comment and brainstorm some ideas. Then, use the outline to generate your ideas.

Professor Courtland

Lately, numerous scientific discoveries, especially in medicine, chemistry, and physics, have been made. Their discoverers have earned huge sums of money by selling the results of their discoveries. Here is a question to consider: Should important discoveries be shared for the benefit of humanity? Or should people and governments be allowed to profit from them? Why do you think so?

Words & Phrases

chemistry (n) the science concerned with the compositions, structures, and properties of substances
sum (n) an amount

result (n) an effect; a consequence of an action
share (v) to use or experience with others
profit (v) to make money

✦ Outline for Brainstorming

Share Important Discoveries or Profit from Them

Share Important Discoveries		Profit from Important Discoveries	
Reason 1	**Reason 2**	**Reason 1**	**Reason 2**
Duty to share discoveries with others	Amazing pharmaceuticals → many cannot afford	People spent $ and time → have right to get back investments	Only patent discoveries for limited number of years

B Read the following comments by two students and complete the summary notes.

Sophie

When people make discoveries that could benefit millions of people, it is their duty to share their discoveries with the world. For instance, some amazing pharmaceuticals have been discovered, but some people cannot acquire them because the costs are too high. As a result, these people die when they should live. Unfortunate events like this should never occur.

Words & Phrases

duty (n) an obligation; a task a person must do
amazing (adj) incredible
pharmaceutical (n) a medicine; a medication

acquire (v) to get; to purchase
unfortunate (adj) unlucky

Summary Notes: Sophie

Share Important Discoveries

1 Make important ¹⁾ .... → affect ²⁾ ....
 • ³⁾ .... to share w/world

2 Are some ⁴⁾ ....
 • People ⁵⁾ .... → costs = ⁶⁾ ....
 • People ⁷⁾ .... as result

Stuart

People spend vast sums of money and sometimes years of their lives to make scientific discoveries. They have every right to attempt to monetize their discoveries to recover their investments of time and money. Let us remember that they can only patent their discoveries for a limited number of years. Then, anyone has the right to use them.

Words & Phrases

vast (adj) very large or great; enormous
monetize (v) to use something to make money from it
recover (v) to get back

investment (n) something, often money, spent in order to make a profit
patent (v) to gain the exclusive right to sell, make, or use an invention

Summary Notes: Stuart

Profit from Important Discoveries

1 People spend $ and years to ¹⁾ ....
 • Have right to ²⁾ ....
 • ³⁾ .... investments of ⁴⁾ ....

2 Can only ⁵⁾ .... for ⁶⁾ .... of years
 • Anyone can ⁷⁾ .... later

Organization Review the outline and the summary notes on the previous pages and then complete each chart.

● Supporting Sophie's Opinion

Introduction	1 While I understand _____ , Sophie _____ .
Body 1	2 The first reason is that _____ . 3 For instance, _____ .
Body 2	4 The second reason is that _____ _____ . 5 These new discoveries _____ . 6 Think about _____ .
Conclusion	7 These two reasons are why _____ .

● Supporting Stuart's Opinion

Introduction	1 I disagree _____ .
Body 1	2 When people _____ , they _____ . 3 There is _____ .
Body 2	4 Something else to think about is _____ _____ . 5 After all, _____ ? 6 When _____ , human knowledge _____ . 7 This will _____ .
Conclusion	8 We should therefore _____ .

Exercise 2 Follow the directions and write a response. You can refer to the outline and the summary notes.

Q Your professor is teaching a class on sociology. Write a post responding to the professor's question.

In your response you should:

- express and support your opinion
- make a contribution to the discussion

An effective response will contain at least 100 words. You will have 10 minutes to write it.

Professor
Rolfson

I would like you to think about social media. Billions of people everywhere use it. It has obvious advantages but also some disadvantages. In fact, some people argue that it can be harmful to children because of its drawbacks. Consider this: Children should not be allowed to use social media. Do you agree or disagree? Why or why not?

📖 **Words & Phrases**

obvious adj clear; apparent; easy to see
advantage n a benefit
disadvantage n an unfavorable or poor condition; a condition that makes success difficult to achieve

argue v to provide reasons either for or against something
drawback n an unfavorable feature; a disadvantage

✦ **Outline for Brainstorming**

> **Do Not Allow Children to Use Social Media**

Agree	Disagree
Reason Can become addicted	**Reason** Can communicate w/others
Example Bro and sis spend time on social media + neglect homework	**Example** Talk to friends and relatives

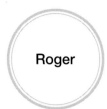

Roger

I wholeheartedly agree that children should not be permitted to use social media. I have a younger brother and a younger sister. Both are addicted to social media. They constantly upload pictures and post updates on their social media pages while neglecting their homework and chores. They, and other children, are clearly too irresponsible to use social media.

Wilma

There is no need to ban children from social media. In fact, they can benefit a lot from it. For instance, they can learn how to use a computer and also communicate with friends and relatives. While some might overuse it, their parents can intervene in those cases. Prohibiting all children from using social media would be an overreaction.

🔍 Words & Phrases

wholeheartedly adv completely devoted or dedicated to something

addicted adj having a compulsive behavior that causes problems

update n current information; new information about something

chore n a small household task

irresponsible adj lacking a sense of reliability

communicate v to pass information back and forth

relative n a person connected to another by blood or marriage

overuse v to use something too much

intervene v to interfere with; to interrupt

overreaction n a reaction that is too strong

✍️ Summary Notes

Roger
1 Have younger bro and sis
• 1) _____
• Upload pictures and post updates
• 2) _____
2 Too irresponsible for social media

Wilma
1 Can benefit from it
• Learn to use a computer
• 1) _____
2 If overuse, parents intervene
• 2) _____

Self-Evaluation Check your response by answering the following questions.

	Yes	No
1 Did you address the professor's question?	☐	☐
2 Did you refer to the comments by the two students?	☐	☐
3 Did you express your own opinion?	☐	☐
4 Did you provide examples to support your opinion?	☐	☐
5 Did you organize your response well?	☐	☐
6 Did you use correct grammar?	☐	☐
7 Did you use correct punctuation?	☐	☐
8 Did you spell all of the words correctly?	☐	☐

Exercise 1 Follow the directions in each step.

Brainstorming & Outlining

A Read the professor's comment and brainstorm some ideas. Then, use the outline to generate your ideas.

Professor
McCloud

We will discuss access to medicines in our next class. I would like you to consider this: There are numerous medicines that have been discovered. However, some are difficult for people to acquire. Do you think certain medicines should only be available through prescriptions? Or should people be able to buy whichever medications they want? Why?

Words & Phrases

access n freedom to obtain or use something
numerous adj very many
prescription n written permission to get and use a certain medicine

whichever adj no matter which
medication n medicine

✦ **Outline for Brainstorming**

The Availability of Certain Medicines

Only through Prescriptions		Available to All	
Reason 1	**Reason 2**	**Reason 1**	**Reason 2**
Medicines potent → get addicted	Serious side effects to some medicines	Let drugstores sell everything	Pharmacists should provide info

B Read the following comments by two students and complete the summary notes.

Florence

Some medicines these days are extremely potent and should only be available after they are prescribed by a licensed doctor. People taking these medications can become addicted to them and suffer serious side effects as well. It is critical that medicines like these be regulated to prevent people from suffering any harm.

📖 **Words & Phrases**

potent adj powerful; very strong
licensed adj having a license to engage in a certain type of business

side effect n a secondary effect of a drug that is typically harmful
critical adj important
regulate v to be under the control of the law

🖊 **Summary Notes: Florence**

> **Only through Prescriptions**
>
> **1** Some medicines [1)] ....
> - Should only be [2)] .... by [3)] ....
>
> **2** Can get [4)] .... to medicines
> - Suffer serious [5)] ....
> - Must [6)] .... medicines
> - Prevent people from [7)] ....

Arnold

I have no problem with people taking any medicine that they want to. Drugstores should be allowed to sell every medicine they have even without a prescription. Pharmacists should, however, be required to advise individuals of two things: how to take the medicine properly and what side effects the medicine could cause.

📖 **Words & Phrases**

drugstore n a store that sells medicine
pharmacist n a healthcare professional who provides medicine to people

advise v to recommend a course of action to someone
properly adv correctly
cause v to make happen

🖊 **Summary Notes: Arnold**

> **Available to All**
>
> **1** Okay to [1)] .... want to
> - Let [2)] .... sell every medicine
> - No need for [3)] ....
>
> **2** Requirements for [4)] ....
> - Advise how to [5)] ....
> - Provide info on [6)] ....

Review the outline and the summary notes on the previous pages and then complete each chart.

● **Supporting Florence's Opinion**

Introduction	1 This is _____, but I know _____.
Body 1	2 I am like Florence and _____. 3 As Florence notes, _____. 4 This is _____. 5 People who _____.
Body 2	6 Something else to think about is that _____. 7 By that, I mean that _____ _____. 8 Doctors _____, so they _____.
Conclusion	9 That is why _____.

● **Supporting Arnold's Opinion**

Introduction	1 Arnold is correct that _____.
Body 1	2 If _____, any customer _____. 3 Many countries _____. 4 The people _____. 5 People in my country _____.
Body 2	6 In addition, _____. 7 They should not _____. 8 That is _____.
Conclusion	9 Clearly, _____.

Follow the directions and write a response. You can refer to the outline and the summary notes.

 Q Your professor is teaching a class on health. Write a post responding to the professor's question.

In your response you should:

- express and support your opinion
- make a contribution to the discussion

An effective response will contain at least 100 words. You will have 10 minutes to write it.

Professor
Gustav

I would like for everyone to think about health care. In recent times, the price of health care has risen dramatically. Some people receive bills for thousands of dollars after hospital stays and operations. This is causing financial strain on many families. Consider this: All health care should be free. Do you agree or disagree? Why or why not?

Words & Phrases

health care n efforts made to restore a person's physical and mental condition
dramatically adv suddenly and extremely

bill n an itemized list showing how much money a person owes for a good or service
operation n an invasive medical procedure; surgery
strain n excessive physical or mental tension

✦ **Outline for Brainstorming**

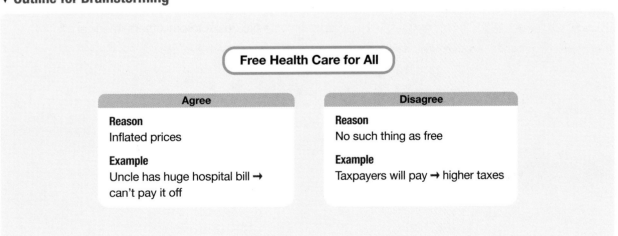

Free Health Care for All

Agree	Disagree
Reason Inflated prices	**Reason** No such thing as free
Example Uncle has huge hospital bill ➜ can't pay it off	**Example** Taxpayers will pay ➜ higher taxes

Ivan

I agree that health care should be free. Recently, my uncle was hospitalized for a week. He had no medical insurance, so his bill was more than 90,000 dollars. He has no way to pay off this inflated price. Numerous people around the country face similar situations. With free health care, they would not have to worry about expensive bills.

Caroline

I sympathize with people who have enormous medical bills, but I disagree with the statement. Free health care really is not free. Someone has to pay for it, and that someone is the country's taxpayers. If free health care happens here, taxes will go up to pay doctors and hospitals. I have no desire to pay for other people's medical care.

Words & Phrases

hospitalize v to put into a hospital as a patient
medical insurance n insurance that covers hospital or doctor's bills
pay off v to pay a bill in full
inflated adj expanded or increased to an abnormal level
face v to deal with

sympathize v to share in a person's bad feelings
enormous adj huge; very large
taxpayer n a person who pays taxes
desire n an urge
medical care n treatment from a doctor

Summary Notes

Ivan

1 Uncle hospitalized for week
- No medical insurance
- Bill = more than $90,000
- 1) ....

2 Numerous people face similar situations
- 2) ....

Caroline

1 1) ....
- Someone must pay
- Someone = country's taxpayers

2 Taxes will go up
- 2) ....
- No desire to pay others' medical bills

	Yes	No
1 Did you address the professor's question?	☐	☐
2 Did you refer to the comments by the two students?	☐	☐
3 Did you express your own opinion?	☐	☐
4 Did you provide examples to support your opinion?	☐	☐
5 Did you organize your response well?	☐	☐
6 Did you use correct grammar?	☐	☐
7 Did you use correct punctuation?	☐	☐
8 Did you spell all of the words correctly?	☐	☐

Actual Test

Actual Test 01

Writing Section Directions

02-01

In this section, you will be able to demonstrate your ability to use writing to communicate in an academic environment. There will be two writing tasks.

In the first task, you will read a passage about an academic topic; you will have 3 minutes to read it. Then you will listen to a lecture about the same topic. After that, you will have **20 minutes** to combine/summarize what you have listened to and read.

For the second task, you will read an online discussion. A professor has posted a question about a topic, and some classmates have responded with their ideas. You will then write a response that contributes to the discussion. You will have **10 minutes** to write your response.

Your responses will be scored on your ability to write correctly, clearly, and coherently, as well as on your ability to respond to the questions as fully as possible.

Now, listen to the directions for the first writing task.

02-02

Writing Based on Reading and Listening
Directions

For this task, you will have three minutes to read a passage about an academic topic. A clock at the top of the screen will show how much time you have to read. You may take notes while you read. You will be able to see the reading passage again when it is time for you to write. You may use your notes to help you answer the question.

You will then have **20 minutes** to write a response to a question that asks you about the relationship between the lecture you have heard and the reading passage. Try to answer the question as completely as possible using information from the reading passage and the lecture. The question does **not** ask you to express your personal opinion.

Typically, an effective response will be 150 to 225 words. Your response will be judged on the quality of your writing and on the completeness and accuracy of the content.

Now you will see the reading passage for 3 minutes. Remember that it will be available to you again while you are writing. Immediately after the reading time ends, the lecture will begin, so keep your headset on until the lecture has ended.

Task **1**

While the modern age has led to many improvements in people's lifestyles, one negative aspect has emerged. Namely, the cost of raising children in the United States has ballooned. In fact, raising a child costs more in the United States than in any other country on the Earth.

According to a recent study, on average, parents must pay approximately 310,000 dollars to feed, clothe, and educate their children from the day they are born until they graduate from university at approximately the age of twenty-one. For many families, the costs are even higher since they send their children to expensive private schools and universities, some of which charge more than 80,000 dollars a year for tuition and room and board. This number does not include travel or toys and other playthings, which can also be expensive.

Incredibly, rearing children in the U.S. requires about a third more money than in other Western countries such as France and Spain. One reason for this is the limited socialism found in many European countries, where parents do not have to pay tuition for their children to attend schools. Additionally, while the standard of living is lower in these countries than in the U.S., prices are also cheaper, a big advantage that enables parents to save more money.

Finally, there is the matter of what parents spend their money on. Parents in most countries use the majority of money dedicated to their children on necessities like clothes and food. However, Americans typically spend money on items people from other countries would consider excessive. For example, American parents expend considerable amounts of money on private tutoring in education, music, and athletics. They also pay extremely high amounts for health care for their children. Altogether, it makes bringing up American children very expensive.

02-03

Directions You have 20 minutes to plan and write your response. Your response will be judged on the basis of the quality of your writing and on how well your response presents the points in the lecture and their relationship to the reading passage. Typically, an effective response will be 150 to 225 words.

Question Summarize the points made in the lecture, being sure to specifically explain how they answer the problems raised in the reading passage.

Copy　Cut　Paste　　　Word Count　0

While the modern age has led to many improvements in people's lifestyles, one negative aspect has emerged. Namely, the cost of raising children in the United States has ballooned. In fact, raising a child costs more in the United States than in any other country on the Earth.

According to a recent study, on average, parents must pay approximately 310,000 dollars to feed, clothe, and educate their children from the day they are born until they graduate from university at approximately the age of twenty-one. For many families, the costs are even higher since they send their children to expensive private schools and universities, some of which charge more than 80,000 dollars a year for tuition and room and board. This number does not include travel or toys and other playthings, which can also be expensive.

Incredibly, rearing children in the U.S. requires about a third more money than in other Western countries such as France and Spain. One reason for this is the limited socialism found in many European countries, where parents do not have to pay tuition for their children to attend schools. Additionally, while the standard of living is lower in these countries than in the U.S., prices are also cheaper, a big advantage that enables parents to save more money.

Finally, there is the matter of what parents spend their money on. Parents in most countries use the majority of money dedicated to their children on necessities like clothes and food. However, Americans typically spend money on items people from other countries would consider excessive. For example, American parents expend considerable amounts of money on private tutoring in education, music, and athletics. They also pay extremely high amounts for health care for their children. Altogether, it makes bringing up American children very expensive.

Writing for an Academic Discussion
Directions

For this task, you will read an online discussion. A professor has posted a question about a topic, and some classmates have responded with their ideas.

Write a response that contributes to the discussion. You will have **10 minutes** to write your response. It is important to use your own words in the response.

Typically, an effective essay will contain a minimum of 100 words.

Click on **Continue** to go on.

Task 2

Your professor is teaching a class on urban development. Write a post responding to the professor's question.

In your response you should:

- express and support your opinion
- make a contribution to the discussion

An effective response will contain at least 100 words. You will have 10 minutes to write it.

Professor Bannon

In many urban centers, governments are doing poor jobs of maintaining the roads. Government officials often claim they lack enough funds to fix them. They argue that they need to raise money for road repairs. So let me ask you a question: Do you believe that all major roads in cities should be toll roads? Why?

Lucinda

I believe making major roads in cities toll roads is a wonderful idea. However, all the money raised from tolls needs to be spent on the roads themselves. Government officials cannot be allowed to repurpose the money and spend it on different things. Having toll roads would ensure that city roads are in good condition, which would benefit countless people.

Walter

I am so tired of governments attempting to seize more and more hard-earned money from people. We already pay enough taxes, but now the government wants us to pay more just to use the roads? I simply cannot accept that. If the government would stop wasting money, it would have plenty of funds to maintain the roads.

Copy   Cut   Paste   Word Count   0

Actual Test 02

02-04

Writing Section Directions

In this section, you will be able to demonstrate your ability to use writing to communicate in an academic environment. There will be two writing tasks.

In the first task, you will read a passage about an academic topic; you will have 3 minutes to read it. Then you will listen to a lecture about the same topic. After that, you will have **20 minutes** to combine/summarize what you have listened to and read.

For the second task, you will read an online discussion. A professor has posted a question about a topic, and some classmates have responded with their ideas. You will then write a response that contributes to the discussion. You will have **10 minutes** to write your response.

Your responses will be scored on your ability to write correctly, clearly, and coherently, as well as on your ability to respond to the questions as fully as possible.

Now, listen to the directions for the first writing task.

Writing Based on Reading and Listening Directions

For this task, you will have three minutes to read a passage about an academic topic. A clock at the top of the screen will show how much time you have to read. You may take notes while you read. You will be able to see the reading passage again when it is time for you to write. You may use your notes to help you answer the question.

You will then have **20 minutes** to write a response to a question that asks you about the relationship between the lecture you have heard and the reading passage. Try to answer the question as completely as possible using information from the reading passage and the lecture. The question does **not** ask you to express your personal opinion.

Typically, an effective response will be 150 to 225 words. Your response will be judged on the quality of your writing and on the completeness and accuracy of the content.

Now you will see the reading passage for 3 minutes. Remember that it will be available to you again while you are writing. Immediately after the reading time ends, the lecture will begin, so keep your headset on until the lecture has ended.

Task **1**

One of the most controversial aspects of law enforcement these days is speed cameras. These are cameras that are installed at various places and then used to monitor the speeds of passing drivers. Equipped with radar detectors, they take pictures of speeders, which then results in violators being sent a speeding ticket that they must pay some time later. While many people dislike speed cameras, they are actually beneficial to society.

For one, they have made the roads safer. While there are sometimes signs that indicate that speed cameras are nearby, most of the time, they are hidden from view. Therefore, if drivers feel or know that there is a speed camera in the vicinity, they often drive slower since the price of speeding tickets can be two hundred dollars or higher. Slower speeds mean fewer accidents, so speed cameras are already helping protect people.

Second of all, because of speed cameras, police officers do not have to waste much of their time finding speeders. This frees the police to do the more important aspects of their job, such as catching criminals and helping keep the public safe. In fact, thanks to the success of speed cameras, more and more are being installed, so in the future, police officers may never have to issue any speeding tickets at all.

Finally, because speed cameras provide hard evidence that an individual was, in fact, speeding, fewer people are protesting their tickets in court. This decrease in complaints is starting to free up traffic courts, which are constantly backlogged with cases. So instead of challenging their tickets, most violators, when they receive a picture of their transgression in the mail, simply write a check and pay their fine.

02-06

VOLUME HELP NEXT

Directions You have 20 minutes to plan and write your response. Your response will be judged on the basis of the quality of your writing and on how well your response presents the points in the lecture and their relationship to the reading passage. Typically, an effective response will be 150 to 225 words.

Question Summarize the points made in the lecture, being sure to explain how they cast doubt on specific points made in the reading passage.

Copy   Cut   Paste   Word Count 0

One of the most controversial aspects of law enforcement these days is speed cameras. These are cameras that are installed at various places and then used to monitor the speeds of passing drivers. Equipped with radar detectors, they take pictures of speeders, which then results in violators being sent a speeding ticket that they must pay some time later. While many people dislike speed cameras, they are actually beneficial to society.

For one, they have made the roads safer. While there are sometimes signs that indicate that speed cameras are nearby, most of the time, they are hidden from view. Therefore, if drivers feel or know that there is a speed camera in the vicinity, they often drive slower since the price of speeding tickets can be two hundred dollars or higher. Slower speeds mean fewer accidents, so speed cameras are already helping protect people.

Second of all, because of speed cameras, police officers do not have to waste much of their time finding speeders. This frees the police to do the more important aspects of their job, such as catching criminals and helping keep the public safe. In fact, thanks to the success of speed cameras, more and more are being installed, so in the future, police officers may never have to issue any speeding tickets at all.

Finally, because speed cameras provide hard evidence that an individual was, in fact, speeding, fewer people are protesting their tickets in court. This decrease in complaints is starting to free up traffic courts, which are constantly backlogged with cases. So instead of challenging their tickets, most violators, when they receive a picture of their transgression in the mail, simply write a check and pay their fine.

CONTINUE   VOLUME

Writing for an Academic Discussion
Directions

For this task, you will read an online discussion. A professor has posted a question about a topic, and some classmates have responded with their ideas.

Write a response that contributes to the discussion. You will have **10 minutes** to write your response. It is important to use your own words in the response.

Typically, an effective essay will contain a minimum of 100 words.

Click on **Continue** to go on.

Task 2

Your professor is teaching a class on sociology. Write a post responding to the professor's question.

In your response you should:

- express and support your opinion
- make a contribution to the discussion

An effective response will contain at least 100 words. You will have 10 minutes to write it.

Professor Whittaker

Let's consider sports for a bit. There are both team and individual sports that people participate in. As a general rule, participants in team and individual sports learn different skills and abilities. Which of these two types of sports are better for teenagers to participate in? What skills can they learn by playing them?

Leonardo

I played the team sports football and basketball as a teen. They are clearly superior to individual sports such as golf and bowling and are great for teens. Participants in these sports must learn teamwork. If they do not play well together, their team might lose. Team sports also require strategy, so teens learn to make plans to win games.

Shannon

Both types of sports are good for teens, so I hope all teens participate in them. Nevertheless, individual sports are better for teens. First, players have no one to rely on but themselves to win. So they learn self-reliance. They can also become more confident. After all, if they win, they know they were solely responsible for their victory.

Copy   Cut   Paste   Word Count   0

MEMO

MEMO

Second Edition

How to
Master Skills for the
TOEFL® iBT
WRITING

Answers, Scripts, and Translations

Intermediate

DARAKWON

How to
Master Skills for the

Second Edition

TOEFL® iBT
WRITING · Intermediate

Answers, Scripts,
and Translations

DARAKWON

Unit 01 Technology

Exercise p.14

| Reading |

해석

개인 교통 분야에서 현재 가장 발전 가능성이 있는 것 중 하나는 스마트 카이다. 스마트 카는 첨단 공학이나 인공 지능이 장착된 컴퓨터를 활용하는 차량이다. 스마트 카가 아직 완전히 개발된 것은 아니지만 결국 이는 모든 사람에게 혜택을 가져다 줄 것이다.

스마트 카의 장점 중 하나는 교통 흐름을 원활하게 만들 것이라는 점이다. 스마트 카는 운전 중에 해야 하는 많은 일들을 처리할 수 있기 때문에 차에 탄 사람이 다른 일을 볼 수 있다. 스마트 카는 대부분 자율 주행을 하기 때문에 차량들이 없는 최적의 경로와 그에 합당한 속도를 선택할 수 있다. 이로 인해 이동 시간이 크게 단축되고 교통 흐름도 원활하게 유지될 것이다.

뿐만 아니라 스마트 카는 유지비가 적게 들 것이다. 스마트 카는 거의 전적으로 컴퓨터에 의해 움직이기 때문에 수리를 해야 하는 사소한 문제가 발생하는 경우 컴퓨터가 이를 차주에게 알릴 수 있다. 그러면 차주는 문제가 커져서 과도한 비용이 들기 전에 저렴한 비용으로 차를 수리할 수 있을 것이다.

Note Taking

1) traffic flow faster
2) optimal routes
3) maintenance costs
4) minor problem

| Listening |

Script 🎧 01-02

W Professor: Let's move on to another piece of technology that we are sure to see in the future. I'm talking, of course, about smart cars. Now, don't get too thrilled about them. Yeah, it would be nice to have smart cars do all the driving for us, but they probably won't be as breathtaking as everyone anticipates. Here, uh, let me explain why.

To begin with, you've all seen movies with scenes of smart cars zipping around through traffic, right? Well, unfortunately, that probably won't be what will happen. It's a documented fact that as automobile technology has improved, the amount of traffic has steadily increased. So while we may have cars do the driving for us, you can expect to sit in longer traffic jams. Just because they're smart cars doesn't mean that they'll be smart enough to get you out of a traffic jam.

Second of all, they are not going to be cheap to maintain. "Why?" you may ask. Well, most of the parts of a smart car will be custom made, so due to the manufacturing process, replacing the parts will be expensive. Sure, the labor bill may be cheap, but the bill for the parts is going to be astronomical in some cases. So think about those things before you get too excited about smart cars. Okay?

해석

W Professor: 미래에 만날 것이 확실한 또 다른 기술로 넘어가 보죠. 물론 스마트 카를 말씀드리는 것입니다. 자, 너무 흥분하지는 마세요. 그래요, 스마트 카가 우리를 위해 운전을 해 준다면 멋지겠지만, 아마 여러분들이 기대하는 것만큼 획기적이지는 않을 것입니다. 이제 그 이유를 설명해 드리죠.

먼저, 여러분 모두 영화 속 장면에서 스마트 카들이 차들 사이를 획획 달리는 장면을 보았을 것입니다, 그렇죠? 음, 안타깝지만 아마도 그런 일은 일어나지 않을 거예요. 자동차 기술이 발달할수록 교통량이 꾸준히 증가한다는 점은 입증된 사실입니다. 그래서 자동차가 사람들을 대신해 운전을 하더라도 더 길어진 교통 정체 시간 동안 자리에 앉아 있어야 한다는 점을 예상할 수 있어요. 스마트 카라고 해서 이들이 교통 체증에서 빠져나올 수 있을 만큼 똑똑하다는 얘기는 아니니까요.

두 번째로, 유지 비용이 싸지 않을 것입니다. 왜냐고 물을 수도 있겠군요. 음, 스마트 카의 대다수 부품들은 주문 생산으로 만들어질 것이어서 제조 공정 때문에 부품 교환 비용이 많이 발생할 거예요. 물론 공임은 쌀 수도 있지만 일부 경우에는 부품 교환 비용이 엄청나게 들 것입니다. 따라서 스마트 카에 너무 흥분하기에 앞서 먼저 그러한 문제들을 생각해 보세요. 알겠죠?

Note Taking

1) amount of traffic
2) longer traffic jams
3) custom-made parts
4) astronomical amount of money

| Comparing the Points |

Smart Cars

Reading (Main Points)	Listening (Refutations)
Smart cars will be able to select the best routes and avoid highly traveled roads, which will decrease the amount of travel time for people.	Historically speaking, traffic always becomes worse with each technological development; therefore, smart cars will still get stuck in traffic jams.
Because computers will warn the owners of impending problems, they can fix these problems while they are still minor, which will not require a large amount of money.	Since many of the parts are custom made, they have to be manufactured specially, so the cost of replacing them will be much higher than normal.

Paraphrasing & Summarizing

A

1 Smart cars operate by <u>making use of sophisticated technology as well as computers</u> that can think for themselves to some extent.

2 By doing <u>the majority of the driving</u>, a smart car will enable <u>all the passengers, including the driver, to do other things</u>.

3 The car will decide <u>which way it will go</u> by looking at how many cars are on various roads and by <u>checking the speed limits of the roads</u>.

4 The computers in a smart car will <u>let their owner know anytime there is a problem</u> no matter how small it may be.

5 Because the owner can <u>fix the problem while it is still minor</u>, he will not have to suffer a major problem and therefore <u>have to pay lots of money to fix it</u>.

Summary

Smart cars are not completely developed yet, but they are going to be very important in the future. They will help drivers <u>get to their destinations</u> much faster. They will do this by taking over the driving. This will allow the passengers and the driver to do other things, and it will also ensure that the car takes <u>the fastest route possible</u> by avoiding traffic. In addition, owners will not have to <u>pay high maintenance fees</u>. The car's computers will monitor all possible problems, thereby enabling the owner <u>to fix any problems</u> before they develop into something major. This will then save the owner a lot of money on <u>repair costs</u>.

B

1 Even though people would love to <u>let their cars handle the driving</u>, smart cars will probably not <u>live up to their expectations</u>.

2 It is well known that <u>traffic becomes worse as automobiles become more advanced</u>.

3 The artificial intelligence in smart cars will not be sufficient enough <u>to keep the cars from getting stuck in traffic</u>.

4 It is going to be expensive to <u>put the majority of new parts in smart cars</u> because of the way that <u>many of the parts must be made</u>.

5 Even though <u>it will not cost a lot to pay the mechanic</u> for his actual work, it will still be extremely expensive to <u>pay for the replacement parts</u>.

Summary

While most people are expecting great things from smart cars, they will probably not be quite as wonderful as people think they will be. Even though vehicular technology is constantly improving, traffic actually <u>becomes worse</u> with every improvement. There will probably be more, not fewer, <u>traffic jams</u>. So while the cars will be driving themselves, making it easier on the owners, the trips will actually <u>take longer</u>. In addition, when the cars need to be maintained with <u>replacement parts</u>, the owners will have to pay a lot of money. Since smart cars are custom made, the parts are going to be expensive to replace, thereby requiring their owners to <u>spend excessively</u>.

Synthesizing

1 The reading passage claims that <u>smart cars will be able to choose the best routes to arrive at their destinations quickly</u>, but the professor claims that <u>traffic is going to increase as the technology in cars improves</u>.

2 The author declares that <u>it will take less time to travel and that traffic will always be moving</u>, yet the professor states that <u>there will actually be longer traffic jams than before</u>.

3 In contrast to the statement in the reading claiming that <u>it will be cheap to maintain smart cars</u>, the professor asserts that <u>the manufacturing process involved in creating replacement parts ensures that maintenance costs will be high</u>.

4 Whereas the reading passage asserts that <u>owners will be able to repair their cars cheaply because the problems requiring fixing will be minor</u>, the professor declares that <u>the replacement parts themselves are going to cost an incredible amount of money</u>.

Organization

1 The reading passage and the lecture both discuss <u>aspects of smart cars</u>.

2 However, the professor states that <u>smart cars will not be as great as people expect</u>.

3 She gives two reasons why <u>she believes they will not improve on current vehicles</u>.

4 First, the professor asserts that <u>smart cars will not resemble scenes in movies where they move rapidly through cities</u>.

5 She states that as automobile technology has improved, <u>it has always created more traffic, not less</u>.

6 This contradicts the reading passage, which affirms that <u>smart cars will avoid traffic jams by controlling the routes they drive along</u>.

7 In addition, the professor claims that <u>future traffic jams involving smart cars will be bigger than they currently are.</u>

8 Next, the professor mentions <u>the maintenance costs of smart cars.</u>

9 She declares that <u>most smart car parts are custom made, so they must be specially manufactured, making them incredibly expensive.</u>

10 The reading states that <u>smart cars will tell their owners when they have minor problems, allowing them to be fixed rather cheaply.</u>

11 However, the professor states that while <u>labor fees will not be expensive, any repair work involving spare parts will be.</u>

12 In conclusion, <u>the professor has a dim view of the future of smart cars, which directly contrasts the opinion of the author of the reading passage, who believes smart cars will be very beneficial.</u>

| Writing |

Sample Response

The reading passage and the lecture both discuss aspects of smart cars. However, the professor states that smart cars will not be as great as people expect. She gives two reasons why she believes they will not improve on current vehicles.

First, the professor asserts that smart cars will not resemble scenes in movies where they move rapidly through cities. She states that as automobile technology has improved, it has always created more traffic, not less. This contradicts the reading passage, which affirms that smart cars will avoid traffic jams by controlling the routes they drive along. In addition, the lecture claims that future traffic jams involving smart cars will be bigger than they currently are.

Next, the professor mentions the maintenance costs of smart cars. She declares that most smart car parts are custom made, so they must be specially manufactured, making them incredibly expensive. The reading states that smart cars will tell their owners when they have minor problems, allowing them to be fixed rather cheaply. However, the professor states that while labor fees will not be expensive, any repair work involving spare parts will be.

In conclusion, the professor has a dim view of the future of smart cars, which directly contrasts the opinion of the author of the reading passage, who believes smart cars will be very beneficial.

해석

지문과 강의 모두 스마트 카의 측면에 관해 논의한다. 하지만 교수는 스마트 카가 사람들이 기대하는 것만큼 대단하지는 않을 것이라고 주장한다. 그녀는 스

마트 카가 현재의 차량들보다 우수하지는 않을 것이라고 생각하는 두 가지 이유를 제시한다.

첫째, 교수는 스마트 카가 영화 장면에서처럼 도시를 빠르게 질주하지는 않을 것이라고 주장한다. 그녀는 자동차 기술이 발전할수록 항상 교통량이, 적어지는 것이 아니라, 늘어났다고 말한다. 이는 읽기 지문과 상반되는 것으로, 읽기 지문은 스마트 카가 운전 경로를 제어함으로써 교통 정체를 피하게 될 것으로 확신한다. 또한 강의에서는 스마트 카까지 가세한 미래의 교통 체증이 현재보다 심해질 것이라고 주장한다.

다음으로, 교수는 스마트 카의 유지비를 언급한다. 그녀는 대부분의 스마트 카 부품들이 주문 생산되기 때문에 이들은 특별 제작을 해야 해서 그 비용이 엄청날 것이라고 주장한다. 하지만 읽기 지문에는 사소한 문제가 있는 경우 스마트 카가 이를 차주에게 알려 줌으로써 다소 저렴한 비용으로 수리가 가능하다고 나와 있다. 하지만 교수는 공임이 비싸지 않을지라도 추가적인 부품을 필요로 하는 수리의 비용은 비쌀 것이라고 주장한다.

결론적으로 교수는 스마트 카의 미래가 어두울 것이라는 견해를 가지고 있는데, 이는 스마트 카가 매우 유익할 것이라고 생각하는 읽기 지문의 저자와 직접적으로 반대되는 견해이다.

Unit 02 Environmental Science I

Exercise ·· p.22

| Reading |

해석

많은 환경론자들은 생태계에 새로운 종이 유입되는 것을 경계한다. 생태계는 깨지기 쉬우며 외래종이 원래 살던 곳이 아닌 다른 곳으로 유입될 경우 종종 많은 문제를 일으킬 수 있다. 실제로 이들이 새로운 생태계에 침입하면 몇 가지 해로운 효과를 미치는 경우가 많다.

우선 새로운 종의 유입으로 여러 가지 면에서 지역 생태계가 파괴될 수 있다. 우선 새로운 종이 포식자로서 다른 토착종들을 잡아먹으면 이들이 멸종할 수 있다. 또 다른 측면은 새로운 종이 역내의 귀중한 먹이 자원을 지나치게 소비할 수 있다는 점이다. 이러한 소비로 인해 다른 동물들은 원래 먹던 것만큼의 먹이를 먹을 수 없게 된다. 그 결과 토착종의 수가 감소할 수도 있다.

비자생종이 해를 끼치는 또 다른 측면은 그 지역에 사는 사람들에게 금전적인 손실을 입힌다는 것이다. 이에 대한 한 가지 예는 미 남서부 지역의 메스키트 나무이다. 이 나무는 물이 거의 없는 지역에서 잘 자란다. 그러나 이 식물이 토양의 수분을 다 흡수해 버리기 때문에 주변 지역의 풀은 충분히 성장하지 못하고 죽게 된다. 이로써 역내의 목장주들은 가축 사료비로 추가적인 비용을 지출해야 하기 때문에 금전적인 손실을 보고 있다. 뿐만 아니라 메스키트 나무는 쉽게 번식을 하기 때문에 농부들은 많은 비용을 들여서 자신의 토지에서 이 나무를 제거해야 한다.

Note Taking

1) eat native species
2) enough food
3) Soak up all the water
4) Regenerate very easily

▌ Listening ▌

Script 🎧 01-03

M Professor: Why don't we discuss a few more exotic species before today's class ends? Now, although we've discussed a lot of harmful exotic species, please remember that they are not always detrimental to the local ecosystem. In fact, I could name a few that have actually been, well, beneficial. Don't believe me? Okay, listen to this.

Everyone knows that Kansas is famous for wheat and that Texas is celebrated for cows. Well, they are both, uh, exotic species. And they haven't done any harm to the environment. For example, wheat has not caused the extinction of any local wildlife. It doesn't use up an excessive amount of resources like some exotic species do. And cows, of course, are not predators, so no animals have been killed by them while they graze.

Those are two examples of harmless exotic species. But how about exotic species that are, uh, beneficial? Yeah, it sometimes happens. A perfect case is that of the cane toad, which was introduced for farmers down in Florida, among other places. Cane toads devour many harmful insects, so they keep the bug population down. In addition, since the toads eat so many insects, farmers don't have to use any pesticides that could be dangerous to humans. So cane toads are actually helpful to many people, showing that exotic species sometimes do have benefits.

해석

M Professor: 수업을 끝내기 전에 외래종을 몇 개 더 이야기해 볼까요? 자, 여러 해로운 외래종에 대한 논의를 하기는 했지만, 이들이 항상 지역 생태계에 해를 끼치는 것은 아니라는 점을 기억해 주세요. 사실 실제로, 음, 유익한 몇 가지 종의 이름을 들 수도 있습니다. 못 믿겠어요? 좋아요, 잘 들어 주세요.

캔자스는 밀로 유명하고 텍사스는 소로 유명하다는 것은 누구나 알고 있습니다. 음, 이들은 모두, 어, 외래종이에요. 그리고 이들은 환경에 아무런 해도 끼치지 않습니다. 예를 들어 밀 때문에 멸종한 역내 야생 생물은 없습니다. 일부 외래종처럼 과도한 양의 자원을 소모시키지도 않죠. 그리고 물론 소는 포식 동물이 아니라서 어떤 동물도 풀을 뜯어 먹는 동안 이들에게 잡아먹힌 적이 없습니다.

이 둘은 해를 끼치지 않는 외래종의 예입니다. 하지만, 어, 이로움을 가져다 주는 외래종은 어떨까요? 그래요, 때때로 그런 경우가 있어요. 완벽한 예는 수수두꺼비로, 이는 특히 플로리다 남부 지역의 농부들을 위해 도입이 되었습니다. 이들은 많은 해충을 닥치는 대로 잡아먹어서 해충의 개체수를 낮춰 줍니다. 또한 수수두꺼비가 많은 해충을 잡아먹기 때문에 인간에게 해를 끼칠 수도 있는 살충제를 농부들이 전혀 사용하지 않아도 되죠. 그래서 수수두꺼비는 실제로 많은 사람에게 도움을 주는데, 이는 외래종이 때때로 유익하기도 하다는 점을 보여 줍니다.

✏ Note Taking

1) Wheat
2) Cows
3) cane toad
4) pesticides

▌ Comparing the Points ▌

Exotic Species

Reading (Main Points)	Listening (Refutations)
Exotic species can harm the ecosystem by killing all the native species or by eating their food supply.	Many exotic species, like wheat and cows, do not have any negative effects on their new ecosystems because they do not kill any of the local plant or animal life.
Some nonnative species like the mesquite tree can cause financial damage because of its killing of local plant life or the cost of paying for its removal.	Some exotic species, like the cane toad, which kills bugs and keeps farmers from having to use pesticides that can be harmful to humans, can actually be helpful to people.

▌ Paraphrasing & Summarizing ▌

A

1 When nonnative species go to a new place, they can often cause many problems because most local environments can be disrupted easily.

2 Some nonnative species hunt and kill native species, occasionally to the point of wiping them out entirely.

3 Some native species have to eat less than their normal diet because exotic species are devouring all of their food.

4 Some exotic species are detrimental because they cause locals to lose money.

5 It is expensive for farmers to have mesquite trees eliminated from a plot of land since they grow back fast.

✍ Summary

Because ecosystems can easily be disrupted, most environmentalists do not want animal or plant species introduced to a new area. For example, exotic species might act as predators and kill all of a local species. Or they might simply eat other animals' food sources, which will cause these animals to starve to death. Other exotic species cause significant financial damage. An example of this is the mesquite tree. This tree kills all the local grass, so farmers need to purchase more food for their animals. The trees are also hard to eliminate from the land, so farmers have to spend a lot of money paying for their removal.

B

1 While many exotic species damage their new environments, this is not always the case.

2 It is well known that many farmers grow wheat in Kansas and that many ranchers raise cows in Texas.

3 Cows are harmless creatures that do not do anything to other animals while they are out in the fields.

4 The cane toad in Florida, one of the places the animal was introduced, has actually helped the local environment.

5 Because cane toads eliminate many insects, there is no need to fill the environment with potentially harmful pesticides.

✎ Summary

Many people believe that all exotic species harm their new environments, but that is not necessarily true. Some nonnative plants and animals do not damage their local ecosystems. Two examples of this are Kansas wheat and Texas cows. The wheat has never killed another local species. Likewise, the cows simply graze in their fields and do not harm others. In addition, some exotic species can actually benefit their new homes. The cane toad in Florida is one such example. It kills many insects that eat farmers' crops. Its presence also means that farmers do not have to resort to using any harmful pesticides on their crops. In this case, the cane toad has truly improved the local environment.

Synthesizing

1 The reading declares that nonnative species may become predators and hunt native species to extinction, but the professor claims that the growing of wheat, which is a nonnative species, has not resulted in any species becoming extinct.

2 While the author of the reading passage claims that many exotic species can damage their local environments by eating a significant amount of a food source, the professor states that cows are not dangerous to their new environments because they have never harmed any other species.

3 In opposition to the claim that mesquite trees kill the local grass so that farmers have to pay more for feed, the professor asserts that some exotic species, like the cane toad, are beneficial because they eat lots of harmful insects.

4 Contrasting the reading's assertion that eliminating mesquite trees is expensive to farmers, the professor believes that cane toads are helpful to humans because the land does not require potentially harmful pesticides since the animals eat insects.

Organization

1 The reading passage and the lecture are both about exotic species, but they disagree as to the effects on their new environments.

2 The professor believes that exotic species have no effect on their environment or are beneficial.

3 However, the reading passage believes they are harmful.

4 The professor first states that many exotic species, like Kansas wheat and Texas cows, do not negatively affect the environment.

5 He claims that neither one of them has caused the extinction of any species.

6 The reading, however, disagrees and claims that many nonnative species are predators, so they hunt some animals to extinction.

7 In addition, they sometimes eat all of an area's food supply, which causes local animals to die of starvation.

8 The professor also asserts that some exotic species can be beneficial to their new environment.

9 He cites the example of the cane toad in Florida.

10 He claims that cane toads eat insects, so they keep the bug population down and allow farmers not to use dangerous insecticides.

11 However, the reading claims that some exotic species, like the mesquite tree, cause financial harm to farmers.

12 The reading states that since mesquite trees kill grass, farmers must pay more for animal feed.

13 It is also expensive to remove them from the land.

14 Clearly, the reading passage and the lecture disagree with one another with regard to the value of exotic species.

Writing

Sample Response

The reading passage and the lecture are both about exotic species, but they disagree as to the effects on their new environments. The professor believes that exotic species have no effect on their environment or are beneficial. However, the reading passage believes they are harmful.

The professor first states that many exotic species, like Kansas wheat and Texas cows, do not negatively affect the environment. He claims that neither one of them has caused the extinction of any species. The reading, however, disagrees and claims that many nonnative species are predators, so they hunt some animals to extinction. In addition, they sometimes eat all of an area's food supply, which causes local animals to die of starvation.

The professor also asserts that some exotic species can be beneficial to their new environment. He cites the example of the cane toad in Florida. He claims that cane toads eat insects, so they keep the bug population down and allow farmers not to use dangerous insecticides. However, the reading claims that some exotic species, like the mesquite tree, cause financial harm to farmers. The reading states that since mesquite trees kill grass, farmers must pay more for animal feed. It is also expensive to remove them from the land.

Clearly, the reading passage and the lecture disagree with one another with regard to the value of exotic species.

해석

읽기 지문과 강의는 모두 외래종에 관한 것이지만 외래종이 새로운 환경에 미치는 영향에 대해서는 견해를 달리한다. 교수는 외래종이 환경에 영향을 미치지 않거나 유익하다고 생각한다. 하지만 읽기 지문은 외래종이 유해하다고 생각한다.

교수는 먼저 캔자스의 밀이나 텍사스의 소와 같이 많은 외래종이 환경에 부정적인 영향을 미치지 않는다고 말한다. 그는 그 둘 모두 어떠한 종도 멸종시키지 않았다고 주장한다. 하지만 읽기 지문은 그에 동의하지 않고 많은 비자생종이 포식자이기 때문에 일부 동물을 사냥해서 이들을 멸종시켰다고 주장한다. 또한 이들은 때때로 한 지역의 먹이를 전부 먹어 치워서 역내 동물들을 굶어 죽게 만들기도 한다.

교수는 또한 일부 외래종이 새로운 환경에 도움을 줄 수도 있다고 주장한다. 그는 플로리다의 수수두꺼비를 그 예로 든다. 그는 수수두꺼비가 해충을 잡아먹어서 해충의 수가 줄어들었고 농부들은 위험한 살충제를 사용하지 않게 되었다고 주장한다. 하지만 읽기 지문은 메스키트 나무와 같은 일부 외래종이 농부들에게 금전적인 피해를 입힐 수도 있다고 주장한다. 읽기 지문에는 메스키트 나무가 풀을 죽게 만들어서 농부들이 사료값으로 더 많은 비용을 지불해야 한다고 나와 있다. 또한 땅에서 메스키트 나무를 제거하는 일에도 많은 비용이 든다.

분명 읽기 지문과 강의는 외래종의 가치와 관련해서 서로 다른 견해를 나타낸다.

Unit 03 Sociopolitics

Exercise p.30

| Reading |

해석

미국 정치에서 논란이 되고 있는 한 가지 문제는 휘발유세의 인상에 관한 것이다. 많은 이들은 휘발유세를 인상하면 경제에 도움이 될 것이라고 믿기 때문에 인상을 지지한다. 하지만 휘발유세 인상은 분명 미국 경제에 부정적인 영향을 미칠 것이므로 그러한 믿음은 잘못된 것이다.

우선, 휘발유세 인상은 경제에 해가 될 것이다. 많은 사람들이 자동차로 출근을 한다. 단 몇 퍼센트의 인상만으로도 정부는 사람들의 통근 비용을 증가하게

만들 것이다. 많은 경우 사람들은 이러한 추가 비용을 감당할 수가 없다. 뿐만 아니라 휘발유에 더 많은 비용을 지출한다면 사람들은 다른 제품 구매에 돈을 덜쓰게 될 것이다. 미국 경제는 소비자의 지출에 의해 돌아가기 때문에 소비 감소는 경제에 심각한 피해를 입힐 수 있다.

두 번째로, 휘발유세 인상은 저소득층에 피해를 가져다 줄 것이다. 당연하게도 인상이 이루어지면 휘발유 가격이 상승할 것인데, 이러한 사람들은 휘발유세를 낼 만한 돈을 가지고 있지 않다. 게다가 저소득층의 많은 사람들이 대중 교통이 없는 지역에서 살기 때문에 이들이 외출을 하거나 직장에 나가는 것조차 불가능해질 수 있다. 아무리 좋게 보더라도 재정적인 어려움만 가중될 것이다.

✎ Note Taking

1) people's finances
2) the overall economy
3) more expensive
4) public transportation

| Listening |

Script 🎧 01-04

M Professor: While we're on the topic of taxes, let's discuss another touchy issue. I'm referring, of course, to the gasoline tax. I must say that I'm strongly in favor of raising the gas tax for a number of reasons. Allow me to explain a couple of them.

One argument people always like to use against the gas tax is that it will disrupt the economy. Well, I disagree. For one thing, our economy is way too complex for just one factor to hurt the economy. A raise in percentage points in the gas tax wouldn't in any way dramatically harm our economy. There are also many other factors that are already doing tremendous economic damage. Healthcare expenses and fixing the nation's infrastructure are just two of these.

In addition, let's think about how people with low incomes would be affected. Yes, the gas tax would take money that they can't afford to spend out of their pockets. However, all it takes is a little creativity to solve this problem. For example, the government could give tax breaks to people whose incomes are below a certain level. This would, in a sense, give them a rebate on the gas tax. Or the government could also allow people with lower incomes to pay less money when they go to fill up their cars.

해석

M Professor: 세금 문제를 다루는 김에 또 다른 까다로운 문제에 대해 논의해보죠. 물론 휘발유세를 말씀드리는 것입니다. 저는 여러 가지 이유로 휘발유세 인상을 강력히 지지하는 편이에요. 그중 두 가지 이유를 말씀해 드리죠.

사람들이 휘발유세를 반대하는 이유로 항상 언급하는 것 중 하나가 그로 인해 경제가 방해를 받을 것이라는 점입니다. 음, 저는 의견이 다릅니다. 우선 우리 경제는 너무나 복잡해서 단 한 가지 요소가 경제에 피해를 입힐 수 없어요. 휘발유세를 몇 퍼센트 인상한다고 해서 우리 경제가 심각한 피해를 받지는 않을 것입니다. 또한 이미 경제에 엄청난 피해를 끼치고 있는 많은 다른 요소들이 존재해요. 의료비 지출과 국가의 기반 시설 수리가 그중 두 가지죠.

또한 저소득층에게 미치는 영향에 대해서도 생각해 봅시다. 그래요, 휘발유세는 저소득층의 주머니에서 그들이 감당하기 힘든 금액을 빼내 갈 것입니다. 하지만 약간의 창의력만 발휘하면 이러한 문제는 해결할 수 있어요. 예를 들어 정부는 소득이 일정 수준 이하인 사람들에게 세금 감면 혜택을 줄 수도 있습니다. 이는 어떤 의미에서 세금을 환급해 주는 식이 될 거예요. 아니면 저소득층이 자동차 연료를 주입하려고 오는 경우, 정부가 이들에게 낮은 가격을 적용해 줄 수도 있습니다.

✏️ Note Taking

1) very complex
2) health care
3) tax breaks
4) gas stations

▌Comparing the Points▐

Raising the Gasoline Tax

Reading (Main Points)	Listening (Refutations)
Increasing the gasoline tax would be bad for America because it would increase the prices of people's daily commutes and also reduce spending, which would harm the economy.	A rise in the gasoline tax would not hurt the economy since the economy is too big to be affected by it and also because there are other problems like health care and infrastructure that are causing economic damage.
Raising the gasoline tax would harm people with low incomes since they would not be able to afford gas and do not have access to good public transportation.	While a gasoline tax would hurt people with low incomes, the government could give them tax breaks or charge them less for gasoline at gas stations.

▌Paraphrasing & Summarizing▐

A

1 People who think increasing the gasoline tax would not hurt the economy are wrong.

2 If the gas tax increases, it will make getting to work and home more expensive for everyone.

3 More spending on gas will cause people to buy fewer other items.

4 People who do not make much money would not be able to afford gas if the gasoline tax goes up.

5 Those with low salaries who live in areas without buses or subways will not have enough money to get to work or drive to other places.

✏️ Summary

Although some people believe the government should increase the gasoline tax, it would actually harm the economy. First, many people use their cars to drive to work. Raising the gas tax would make these trips more expensive. And then people would spend less money buying other products. The American economy needs people to buy things, or else it will start getting bad. In addition, a high gasoline tax would be bad for people who earn low salaries. They might not even be able to afford to drive to work. Since they cannot take public transportation, it would be difficult for them to get around.

B

1 In my view, there are many reasons why the gasoline tax should be raised.

2 Due to the complexity of the economy, one factor alone cannot cause it to decline.

3 Many other things, such as the costs of medical expenses and repairing roads and bridges, are already harming the economy.

4 The government could lower taxes on people who make less than a certain amount of money.

5 It might be possible to charge poor people less money at gas stations.

✏️ Summary

The professor fully supports increasing the gasoline tax for a couple of different reasons. First, he does not agree with arguments that a higher gas tax would harm the economy. Since the American economy is so big and complex, it would be impossible for an increased gas tax to damage it. Likewise, issues like health care and repairing infrastructure are already causing lots of damage to the economy. Second, while people with low incomes would be hurt by an increased tax, there are ways to avoid this pain. The government could give them tax breaks to compensate them for the increase in taxes. Or they could simply pay less when they go to fill up their cars.

▌Synthesizing▐

1 The reading passage declares that increasing the gasoline tax would cause people to pay more money to get to work and home, but the professor claims that the gas tax would not hurt the American economy due to its complexity.

2 The reading claims that people spending more money on gas will purchase fewer other products, yet the professor argues that there are more pressing issues to

the economy, such as healthcare expenses and fixing the country's infrastructure.

3   In response to the claim that poor people do not have enough money to pay a more expensive gas tax, the professor states that people with low incomes could be offered tax breaks by the government.

4   While the reading asserts that due to a lack of public transportation, poor people would not be able to get to work if the gas tax went up, the professor maintains that these individuals could be allowed to pay lower rates for gasoline at gas stations.

| Organization |

1   The professor firmly disagrees with the reading passage, which states that increasing the gasoline tax would harm the economy.

2   Instead, the professor feels that this would not have a negative effect on the economy.

3   To begin with, the reading passage declares that an increase in the gasoline tax would make people's commutes cost more.

4   The author also mentions that people would therefore spend less money.

5   Since the American economy needs people to spend money to remain strong, it would start to go into decline.

6   However, the professor believes the gas tax could not harm the economy since it is too complex to be affected by one tax.

7   Plus, a gas tax's effects cannot compare to healthcare costs and the repair of the country's infrastructure, which are already damaging the current economy.

8   The reading also states that people with low incomes will not be able to afford gas and may not be able to go to work or anywhere else.

9   The professor mentions that the government could simply give people tax breaks.

10 He also thinks that people with low incomes could pay less when they go to gas stations.

11 The professor and the reading passage are definitely in disagreement over the gasoline tax, and both provide a couple of reasons in defense of their arguments.

| Writing |

Sample Response

The professor firmly disagrees with the reading passage, which states that increasing the gasoline tax would harm the economy. Instead, the professor feels that this would not have a negative effect on the economy.

To begin with, the reading passage declares that an increase in the gasoline tax would make people's

commutes cost more. The author also mentions that people would therefore spend less money. Since the American economy needs people to spend money to remain strong, it would start to go into decline. However, the professor believes the gas tax could not harm the economy since it is too complex to be affected by one tax. Plus, a gas tax's effects cannot compare to healthcare costs and the repair of the country's infrastructure, which are already damaging the current economy.

The reading also states that people with low incomes will not be able to afford gas and may not be able to go to work or anywhere else. The professor mentions that the government could simply give people tax breaks. He also thinks that people with low incomes could pay less when they go to gas stations.

The professor and the reading passage are definitely in disagreement over the gasoline tax, and both provide a couple of reasons in defense of their arguments.

해석

교수는 휘발유세 인상이 경제에 피해를 입힐 것이라는 읽기 지문 내용에 전적으로 반대한다. 대신 교수는 경제에 그로 인한 부정적인 영향이 미치지 않을 것으로 생각한다.

우선 읽기 지문에는 휘발유세 인상으로 사람들의 통근 비용이 늘어날 것이라고 나와 있다. 또한 저자는 그 결과로 사람들의 소비가 줄어들 것이라고 언급한다. 미국 경제는 사람들이 소비를 해야 탄탄하게 유지되기 때문에 그로 인해 경기가 하락하기 시작할 것이다. 하지만 교수는 미국 경제가 너무 복잡해서 한 가지 세금에 의해 영향을 받지는 않으므로 휘발유세가 미국 경제에 피해를 줄 수는 없다고 생각한다. 또한 휘발유세의 효과는 이미 현 경제에 피해를 입히고 있는 의료비 및 국가 기반 시설 수리 비용의 경우와 비교될 수 없다.

읽기 지문은 또한 저소득층이 휘발유 값을 감당하기가 힘들 것이며 직장이나 다른 어떤 곳에도 갈 수 없게 될 것이라고 주장한다. 교수는 정부가 이들에게 세제 혜택을 줄 수 있을 것이라고 언급한다. 그는 또한 소득이 낮은 사람들이 주유소 방문 시 이들에게 낮은 가격을 적용할 수 있을 것이라고 생각한다.

교수와 읽기 지문은 휘발유세에 관련해서 완전히 상반된 견해를 나타내며, 둘 다 각자의 주장에 대해 두 가지 이유를 제시한다.

Unit 04   Environmental Science II

Exercise p.38

| Reading |

해석

산불의 위험 때문에 일부 산림 감시원들은 숲을 관리하는 새로운 방법을 도입하기 시작했다. 이 방법은 처방화입이라고 불린다. 이들이 하는 일은 실제로 숲에 불을 지펴서 다양한 종류의 나무나 기타 식물들을 태우는 것이다. 안타깝게도 처방화입은 각기 다른 여러 가지 이유에서 효과적인 방법이 아니다.

첫째 산불은 통제가 극도로 어렵다. 산림 감시원은 막대한 주의를 기울인다고 주장하지만 처방화입이 통제를 벗어날 수도 있다. 이러한 일은 실제로 몇 차례 발생한 적이 있다. 감시원들이 불을 통제할 수 없었기 때문에 일반적인 산불이 발생했을 때보다 훨씬 더 큰 피해가 발생했다. 사실 산불은 예측이 불가능하다. 감시원들은 한 지역만 태우고 싶어할 수 있지만 산불의 예측 불가능성 때문에 결국 다른 지역까지 불에 타게 된다.

또한 처방화입의 비용도 싸지 않다. 산불을 피우고 통제하는데 많은 비용이 든다. 이 과정에는 다수의 인원과 장비가 필요하기 때문에 인건비와 장비 사용료를 지불해야 한다. 게다가 산불이 통제 불가능한 상태로 번지기 시작하면 이를 다시 진압하기까지 훨씬 더 많은 비용이 든다. 모든 점을 고려해 볼 때 처방화입은 많은 단점을 지니고 있으며 이를 실행해서는 안 된다.

✏ Note Taking

1) regular forest fires
2) Unpredictable
3) people and equipment
4) burning uncontrollably

Listening

Script 🎧 01-05

M Professor: We all know that forest fires can cause lots of damage to the environment. Remember that one we had last year? Well, the forest is just now starting to recover. However, some environmentalists actually believe that starting forest fires is effective. Imagine that! It's called prescribed burning, and here are its advantages.

First, unlike a regular forest fire, which often burns uncontrollably, prescribed burning can be handled. Park rangers are able to manage exactly where the fire burns and even what plants and trees it burns down. There are many different prescribed burning experts and programs, so park rangers make sure to consult them before they commence with the burning. Even if the fire starts burning unpredictably, they have methods to ensure that the fire does not get out of their control and burn the wrong places.

Second, there are always fires in forests. They actually help rejuvenate the forests. However, natural forest fires can cause up to ten times the damage prescribed burning does. Not only that, but natural forest fires can also get into human settlements, burn down houses and other buildings, and even kill people. By using prescribed burning, authorities can control exactly what gets burned while keeping the fire on a small scale. So they can help the forest recover yet prevent it from entirely burning down.

해석

M Professor: 우리 모두는 산불이 환경에 막대한 피해를 줄 수 있다는 점을 알고 있습니다. 지난 해에 일어났던 산불을 기억하나요? 음, 그 숲은 이제 막 회복하기 시작했어요. 하지만 일부 환경론자들은 실제로 산불을 놓는 것이 효과적

이라고 생각합니다. 상상해 보세요! 이를 처방화입이라고 부르는데, 그 장점을 알려 드리겠습니다.

첫째, 종종 제어가 불가능한 일반적인 산불과는 달리 처방화입은 제어가 가능합니다. 산림 감시원들은 산불이 타는 장소와 그로 인해 타게 될 식물 및 나무들을 정확하게 통제할 수 있어요. 여러 다양한 처방화입 전문가와 프로그램들이 있기 때문에 산림 감시원은 화입을 시작하기에 앞서 조언을 들을 수 있습니다. 산불이 예측 불가능하게 번지기 시작하더라도 산불이 통제를 벗어나 엉뚱한 곳을 태우지 않도록 만들 수 있는 방법들도 있죠.

둘째, 숲에서는 항상 산불이 발생합니다. 산불은 실제로 숲의 회생에 도움을 주어요. 하지만 자연적인 산불은 처방화입에 비해 최고 10배의 피해를 일으킬 수 있어요. 그뿐만 아니라 자연적인 산불은 인간의 주거지로 번져서 주택을 태우고 사람들의 목숨을 앗아갈 수도 있죠. 처방화입을 이용하면 관계 당국이 적은 규모로 산불을 유지하면서 불에 타는 것을 정확히 제어할 수 있습니다. 따라서 숲을 회복시키면서 숲이 완전히 타는 것을 막을 수가 있어요.

✏ Note Taking

1) where fires burn
2) get out of control
3) ten times
4) a small scale

Comparing the Points

Prescribed Burning

Reading (Main Points)	Listening (Refutations)
Some prescribed burning fires may get <u>out of control</u>, which makes them burn more land than was planned and makes them <u>too unpredictable to control</u>.	Park rangers consult experts to make sure that their fires do not burn out of control, and if the fires <u>become unpredictable</u>, they have ways to make sure the fires do not become very bad.
Prescribed burning is not cheap because <u>people's salaries and equipment costs</u> must be paid, and it becomes <u>even more expensive</u> if the fire starts to burn out of control.	Prescribed burning can cause much less damage than <u>natural fires</u> and can help a forest <u>rejuvenate</u> by burning only a small part of it.

Paraphrasing & Summarizing

A

1 There are a lot of reasons why <u>prescribed burning does not really help</u>.

2 Despite the fact that park rangers claim <u>they are careful</u>, a prescribed burning can still suddenly <u>get out of control</u>.

3 Sometimes unpredictable forest fires <u>burn other areas of the forest</u> that the park rangers did not <u>intend to burn</u>.

4 <u>Initiating and controlling a forest fire</u> can be expensive.

5 It can become more expensive to gain back control of a fire once it starts to get out of control.

✎ Summary

Prescribed burning is the practice of starting forest fires on purpose and controlling them so that they burn a small area of the forest. This method, however, has some disadvantages. The first disadvantage is that the fires can sometimes get out of control. Fires are hard to control, and some prescribed burnings have actually gotten out of control and burned unintended places. In fact, rangers often wind up burning other places because they cannot control the fires. The second disadvantage is the cost involved. Paying people's salaries and equipment costs is expensive. In addition, when the fires get out of control, it costs a lot of money to get them back under control.

B

1 According to certain environmentalists, prescribed burning actually works.

2 Park rangers can control prescribed burnings so well that they know which areas will burn and which plants and trees will get burned down.

3 Rangers know various methods to regain control of a fire if it should start burning unpredictably and go into the wrong parts of the forest.

4 Prescribed burnings are ten times less damaging than forest fires.

5 Prescribed burning enables rangers to control the parts of the forest that get burned while not allowing the fire to form on a large scale.

✎ Summary

The professor claims that prescribed burning actually has a number of positive benefits. The first one he cites is that park rangers are able to control these prescribed burnings. Because they consult with experts, they know exactly how to manage these forest fires. In addition, if there is a case where the fire starts to get out of their control, they know a number of different methods to regain control. Second of all, the professor claims that natural forest fires cause ten times the damage that prescribed burnings do. Natural fires also often damage homes and kill people. However, prescribed burnings can take place on a small scale, burn down unwanted areas, and help the forest rejuvenate.

‖ Synthesizing ‖

1 In contrast to the reading passage's claim that prescribed burnings often get out of control, the professor insists that park rangers can determine exactly

where the fire will burn and also which plants and trees it will burn.

2 The author of the reading passage writes that prescribed burnings might burn places that rangers had not intended, yet the professor states that rangers can counter the unpredictable nature of forest fires by using methods to ensure that the fires do not get out of control.

3 The author of the writing declares that a prescribed burning costs a lot of money; however, the professor counters that claim by stating that forest fires can be much more dangerous and can burn homes and kill people.

4 The reading passage states that uncontrollably burning fires are expensive to get back into control, but the professor insists that these fires can be controlled by the authorities and burn on a small scale.

‖ Organization ‖

1 The professor claims that prescribed burnings are beneficial to forests, yet the reading passage declares the opposite.

2 The professor gives several reasons to counter the arguments in the reading passage.

3 First, in contrast to the claim that prescribed burnings can get out of control, the professor says that park rangers can keep these fires under control.

4 He also claims that rangers consult experts, so they know what they are doing.

5 In addition, the professor states that rangers have methods to control unpredictable fires.

6 This is countered by the reading assertion that fires are so unpredictable that they can burn unintended sections of forest.

7 Second, the professor declares that natural forest fires can be ten times as dangerous as prescribed burnings and can even kill people.

8 Meanwhile, the reading says that prescribed burnings are too expensive.

9 The reading also states that it costs a lot of money to get a fire back under control.

10 However, the professor mentions that these fires happen on a small scale; thus, they are able to be controlled and can also help rejuvenate the forest.

11 The professor and the reading clearly disagree with one another with regard to the usefulness of prescribed burnings.

Writing

The professor claims that prescribed burnings are beneficial to forests, yet the reading passage declares the opposite. The professor gives several reasons to counter the arguments in the reading passage.

First, in contrast to the claim that prescribed burnings can get out of control, the professor says that park rangers can keep these fires under control. He also claims that rangers consult experts, so they know what they are doing. In addition, the professor states that rangers have methods to control unpredictable fires. This is countered by the reading assertion that fires are so unpredictable that they can burn unintended sections of forest.

Second, the professor declares that natural forest fires can be ten times as dangerous as prescribed burnings and can even kill people. Meanwhile, the reading says that prescribed burnings are too expensive. The reading also states that it costs a lot of money to get a fire back under control. However, the professor mentions that these fires happen on a small scale; thus, they are able to be controlled and can also help rejuvenate the forest.

The professor and the reading clearly disagree with one another with regard to the usefulness of prescribed burnings

해석

교수는 처방화입이 여러 가지 면에서 숲에 유익하다고 주장하지만 읽기 지문은 그와 반대되는 주장을 하고 있다. 교수는 읽기 지문의 주장을 반박하기 위해 몇 가지 이유를 제시한다.

첫째, 처방화입이 통제를 벗어날 수 있다는 주장에 반대하면서 교수는 산림 감시원들이 이러한 산불을 통제할 수 있다고 말한다. 또한 그는 산림 감시원들이 전문가의 조언을 받기 때문에 자신들이 하는 일을 잘 알고 있다고 주장한다. 게다가 교수는 예상치 못했던 산불을 통제할 수 있는 여러 가지 방법들이 산림 감시원들에게 있다고 주장한다. 이는 산불이 너무나 예측 불가능하기 때문에 의도하지 않았던 지역을 태울 수도 있다는 읽기 지문의 주장과 반대되는 것이다.

둘째, 교수는 자연적인 산불이 처방화입보다 10배 더 위험할 수 있으며 심지어 인명 피해를 가져올 수도 있다고 말한다. 반면에 읽기 지문에는 처방화입의 비용이 너무 높다고 나와 있다. 읽기 지문은 또한 불을 다시 진압하기까지 많은 비용이 든다고 말한다. 하지만 교수는 이러한 산불이 작은 규모로 일어나기 때문에 통제가 가능하고 숲을 회생시키는데 도움이 될 수 있다고 언급한다.

교수와 지문은 처방화입의 유용성과 관련해서 확실히 서로 반대되는 입장을 보이고 있다.

Unit 05 Education I

Exercise p.46

Reading

해석

요즘 많은 학교와 연구 기관들이 점점 더 교육용 DVD와 컴퓨터 동영상에 의존하고 있다. 교재 사용을 선호하는 일부 순수주의자들은 이러한 경향을 극도로 반대하지만 시각 자료에 의존하는 것은 사실 긍정적인 일이다.

먼저 교육 자료는 듣는 사람이 관심을 기울이지 않으면 아무런 쓸모가 없다. 21세기는 비주얼 시대이다. 학생들은 책을 읽는 것보다 DVD 및 컴퓨터 동영상을 시청하는 것에 훨씬 더 익숙하다. 교사들은 시각 자료를 활용함으로써 학생들의 관심을 더 쉽게 끌 수 있다. 또한 DVD와 컴퓨터 동영상은 그래픽과 컴퓨터 애니메이션을 이용하여 어려운 과정 및 아이디어를 보다 쉽게 설명할 수 있다. 이러한 특성 때문에 어려운 주제도 이해하기가 훨씬 쉬워지는데, 이는 학생들의 학습을 진전시키는데 도움이 되는 확실한 장점이다.

또한 DVD와 컴퓨터 동영상은 책보다 훨씬 저렴하다. 많은 시청각 자료들이 10달러 이하의 가격으로 판매되지만 책값은 이것의 2배 내지 3배에 이른다. 많은 학생들의 예산이 빠듯하기 때문에 이러한 경제적 이점은 학생들에게 상당한 도움이 될 것이다. 뿐만 아니라 많은 학교들이 같은 책을 30~40권 혹은 그 이상 구입하는 대신 DVD나 컴퓨터 동영상은 하나만 구매하면 된다. 시청각 자료를 구매함으로써 학교들은 막대한 비용을 아낄 수 있는데, 아낀 비용은 다른 중요한 자료를 구입할 때 쓰일 수 있다.

✏ Note Taking

1) watching visual aids
2) graphics and animation
3) tight budgets
4) purchase just one copy

Listening

Script 🎧 01-06

W Professor: I know many of you prefer watching educational DVDs to reading books. However, I must inform you that books are still much better than watching visual aids. Allow me to educate you as to why.

First, videos are limited by time. You can only impart so much information in a one- or two-hour video. Therefore, the video is likely to be incomplete and not contain all the necessary information. You don't have this issue with books. A 500-page book is filled with much more information than a two-hour DVD. In addition, visual materials are often designed more for entertainment than education. This means they are sometimes highly simplified. You usually can't explain difficult topics on videos. Again, books don't suffer from this problem.

Second of all, visual aids really aren't cheaper than books. Don't believe me? Okay, well, videos of movies are often rather cheap, but this isn't the case for educational materials. They are almost always very pricey, costing between fifty to one hundred dollars a copy.

These prices make them much more expensive than most books. In addition, even if you own an educational DVD, you still have to purchase the DVD player and the television set or the computer, which aren't cheap. And when they break down, as is often the case, they're expensive to repair and also cause annoying delays.

해석

W Professor: 여러분 중 다수는 책을 읽기보다 교육용 DVD를 시청하는 쪽을 더 좋아한다고 생각해요. 하지만 시청각 자료를 보는 것보다 책이 훨씬 낫다는 점을 알려 드리고자 합니다. 그 이유를 말씀 드리죠.

첫째, 동영상에는 시간 제약이 있습니다. 너무 많은 정보를 한 시간 또는 두 시간짜리 동영상에 넣을 수밖에 없죠. 그래서 동영상은 불완전한 경우가 많고, 필요한 모든 정보를 담고 있지 않는 경우도 많아요. 책에는 그러한 문제가 없습니다. 500페이지 책에 2시간짜리 비디오보다 훨씬 많은 정보가 담겨 있어요. 뿐만 아니라 시청각 자료는 교육보다 오락을 위해 만들어진 경우가 많아요. 다시 말해서 동영상은 때때로 크게 단순화되어 있습니다. 보통 어려운 주제는 비디오로 설명할 수가 없어요. 또 다시, 책에서는 이러한 문제를 겪지 않습니다.

둘째, 시청각 자료는 사실 책에 비해 더 싸지 않아요. 믿지 못하겠어요? 좋아요, 음, 영화 동영상은 다소 저렴한 편이지만 교육용 자료는 그렇지가 않습니다. 편당 50에서 100달러 정도인데, 거의 항상 가격이 매우 비싼 편이죠. 이러한 가격 때문에 대부분의 책보다 훨씬 많은 비용이 나가게 됩니다. 뿐만 아니라 교육용 DVD를 가지고 있는 경우에도 DVD 플레이어와 텔레비전, 혹은 컴퓨터를 구입해야 하는데, 이들도 싸지가 않아요. 그리고 흔히 있는 경우로, 이들이 고장나면 수리비도 많이 들고 수업에 차질이 빚어지게 되죠.

✏ Note Taking

1) time restrictions
2) often simplified
3) Educational materials
4) repairs and delays

| Comparing the Points |

Educational Visual Aids

Reading (Main Points)	Listening (Refutations)
Educational visual aids can both get the attention of students and explain difficult topics by using computer graphics or animation.	Visual aids often provide limited information due to time constraints, and they typically rely upon simplified explanations.
Visual aids are cheaper than books, which can be helpful to students on tight budgets, and schools only need one copy, so they can spend their money on other necessities.	Educational visual aids can be much more expensive than books and also require expensive DVD players and TVs or computers, equipment that can sometimes break down.

| Paraphrasing & Summarizing |

A

1 Despite the fact that some traditionalists are opposed to visual aids, they are actually beneficial to use.

2 Teachers can get students to pay attention if they show them DVDs or computer videos.

3 Since they use graphics and animation, visual aids can help students understand even difficult explanations.

4 The prices of books may be two or three times higher than that of DVDs or computer videos.

5 Because schools will save a lot of money by purchasing visual aids, they can use the money to buy other things that they may need.

✎ Summary

The use of visual materials like DVDs and computer videos is something positive even though some people oppose them. The first reason given is that most students are used to watching videos instead of reading books. Therefore, teachers can get their attention more easily. These visual aids can also make difficult concepts simple to understand by using graphics and animation. Second of all, the prices of visual aids are much lower than those of books. This is good for students on tight budgets and for schools since the schools can buy just one DVD or computer video and use the leftover money for other purchases.

B

1 It is preferable to read a book than to watch a DVD or computer video.

2 Visual materials may not contain all the information that they should.

3 Entertaining, not educating, is the purpose of most visual materials.

4 Educational visual materials are more expensive than DVDs of movies.

5 Without purchasing an expensive DVD player and a TV or a computer, you cannot watch a DVD.

✎ Summary

The professor feels that reading books is a much preferable alternative to watching visual materials like DVDs and computer videos. First, she states that visual materials often provide incomplete information because they have to be so short. Books, on the other hand, hold much more information. Visual materials also tend to simplify things since they are more interested in entertaining people instead of educating them. In addition, the professor says that books are actually cheaper than DVDs and computer videos. The reason is that educational visual aids can be much more expensive than movies. Finally, a person with a DVD needs to purchase a DVD player and a TV or a computer, which will cost more money to keep up.

| Synthesizing |

1   The author of the reading declares that visual aids will enable teachers to capture their students' attention; however, the professor counters by saying that videos tend to be incomplete, thereby providing insufficient information.

2   The reading mentions that visual materials can take difficult processes and explain them easily with graphics and computer animation, yet the professor believes these materials are designed to entertain, not to educate, people.

3   In contrast to the reading, which states that books are two or three times more expensive than DVDs and computer videos, the professor claims that educational visual aids are never cheaper than books.

4   While the reading passage mentions that schools can save a lot of money by purchasing visual materials, the professor states that it is not possible to watch a DVD without an expensive DVD player and a TV set or a computer.

| Organization |

1   The professor declares that visual materials are not particularly good.

2   This is in direct contrast to the reading passage, which claims DVDs and computer videos have many benefits.

3   First, the professor states that visual materials are often incomplete while books are not.

4   She says that videos are only a couple of hours long, so they cannot include all of the necessary information that a 500-page book can.

5   The author of the reading, meanwhile, claims that in this visual age, students prefer watching visual materials, which capture their attention.

6   The reading also states that they can make difficult topics easy through graphics and animation.

7   The professor, however, says that visual materials simplify explanations while books do not.

8   Second of all, the professor declares visual materials are more expensive than books while the reading claims the opposite.

9   In addition, the professor says that educational DVDs and computer videos can be fifty to one hundred dollars, yet the reading claims they are two or three times cheaper than books.

10   The reading further says that schools can save money by purchasing visual materials.

11   But the professor states that people still need to purchase expensive and unreliable DVD players and TVs or computers.

12   The professor and the reading passage stand on opposite sides of the debate over the usefulness of visual materials.

| Writing |

Sample Response

The professor declares that visual materials are not particularly good. This is in direct contrast to the reading passage, which claims DVDs and computer videos have many benefits.

First, the professor states that visual materials are often incomplete while books are not. She says that videos are only a couple of hours long, so they cannot include all of the necessary information that a 500-page book can. The author of the reading, meanwhile, claims that in this visual age, students prefer watching visual materials, which capture their attention. The reading also states that they can make difficult topics easy through graphics and animation. The professor, however, says that visual materials simplify explanations while books do not.

Second of all, the professor declares visual materials are more expensive than books while the reading claims the opposite. In addition, the professor says that educational DVDs and computer videos can be fifty to one hundred dollars, yet the reading claims they are two or three times cheaper than books. The reading further says that schools can save money by purchasing visual materials. But the professor states that people still need to purchase expensive and unreliable DVD players and TVs or computers.

The professor and the reading passage stand on opposite sides of the debate over the usefulness of visual materials.

해석

교수는 시청각 자료가 특별히 유익한 것은 아니라고 주장한다. 이는 읽기 지문의 내용과 직접적으로 반대되는 것인데, 읽기 지문은 DVD와 컴퓨터 동영상에 많은 장점이 존재한다고 주장한다.

첫째, 교수는 시청각 자료가 불완전한 경우가 많은 반면 책은 그렇지 않다고 말한다. 그녀는 동영상 길이가 불과 한두 시간에 불과하기 때문에 500페이지의 책에 포함될 수 있는 필요한 정보가 모두 담길 수 없다고 말한다. 반면에 읽기 지문의 저자는 현재의 비주얼 시대에서는 학생들의 관심을 끄는 시청각 자료를 학생들이 더 좋아한다고 주장한다. 또한 읽기 지문에는 시청각 자료가 그래픽과 애니메이션을 통해 어려운 주제를 쉽게 만들 수 있다고 나와 있다. 하지만 교수는 시청각 자료에는 설명이 단순화되어 있으며 책은 그렇지 않다고 말한다.

둘째, 교수는 시청각 자료가 책보다 비싸다고 주장하는 반면 읽기 지문은 그와 반대의 견해를 보인다. 또한 교수는 교육용 DVD 및 컴퓨터 동영상 가격이 50 달러에서 100달러 정도라고 말하지만 읽기 지문에서는 이들이 책에 비해 2배나 3배 더 저렴하다고 나와 있다. 더 나아가 읽기 지문은 시청각 자료의 구매를 통해 학교측이 비용을 절약할 수 있다고 말한다. 그러나 교수는 사람들이 값도 비싸고 신뢰할 수도 없는 DVD 플레이어, TV, 혹은 컴퓨터를 사야 한다고 말한다.

교수와 읽기 지문은 시청각 자료의 유용성에 관한 논쟁에서 정반대의 입장을 취하고 있다.

Unit 06 Business

Exercise p.54

| Reading |

해석

최근에 기업들은 상당수의 직원들이 퇴직 연령인 60세까지 기다리지 않는다는 점에 주목하기 시작했다. 대신 그들은 조기 퇴직을 선택해서 50대일 때 직장을 떠나고 있다. 몇 건의 연구를 진행한 후 기업들은 직원들이 이처럼 갑작스럽게 조기 퇴직을 하는 현상에 두 가지 이유가 있다는 점을 알아냈다.

먼저, 50대의 많은 직원들이 똑같은 고용주를 위해 일을 했고 수 년 혹은 수십 년 동안 똑같은 일을 해 왔다. 따라서 똑같은 업무를 계속 반복하는 과정에서 번아웃을 경험하게 된다. 게다가 매일 반복되는 일과는 더 이상 흥미롭게 느껴지지 않고 대신 엄청난 지루함을 느끼게 된다.

둘째, 나이 든 많은 직원들이 자기 자신과 사내의 젊은 직원들을 비교한다. 이러한 비교가 이루어지면 그 결과는 보통 긍정적인 것이 아니다. 나이가 많은 직원들은 젊은 직원들의 속도를 따라갈 수가 없다. 그렇게 때문에 나이 든 직원들은 젊은 동료 직원들에 비해 자신의 성취도가 낮다고 생각한다. 뿐만 아니라 나이 든 직원들은 자신이 회사의 짐이고 과거만큼 회사에 기여를 하지 못한다는 식으로 생각하기 시작한다. 이러한 자책감 때문에 회사를 나오는 조기 퇴직을 선택하게 된다.

Note Taking

1) burned out
2) daily routines
3) Accomplish less work
4) burdens on their companies

| Listening |

Script 🎧 01-07

W Professor: Now, I'd like to continue talking about how society underutilizes its elderly population. As people live longer and longer, it seems like such a waste for people in their fifties simply to retire and do nothing but play golf or go fishing. So let me give you a couple of suggestions.

Of course, many elderly people don't want full-time jobs. However, a large number would be willing to work part time. This way of working would accomplish a couple of things. First, they wouldn't have to come in every day. This would keep the elderly from getting too worn out to do their jobs. Remember that the elderly

have less energy. Additionally, letting them work part time would keep their minds fresh, which means that they wouldn't become bored with their work.

Here's another idea. I know all of you young people think that you know everything, but your experiences are nothing compared to those of a fifty- or sixty-year-old person. Companies need to do their best to utilize the skills that their older employees have. For example, companies could give these individuals a wider range of duties instead of making them repeat the same tasks over and over. And the companies could consult with their elderly employees more often. This effort would not only make them feel wanted but would also draw upon their many years of experience working at the company.

해석

W Professor: 자, 사회가 얼마나 노년층 인구를 제대로 활용하지 못하고 있는지 계속해서 논의해 보죠. 인간의 수명이 점점 늘어나고 있기 때문에 50대가 은퇴해서 아무것도 하지 않고 골프나 낚시만 한다는 것은 대단한 낭비처럼 보입니다. 따라서 제가 두 가지 제안을 해 볼게요.

물론 많은 노년층들은 정규직 일자리를 원하지 않습니다. 하지만 다수는 기꺼이 시간제 근무를 하려고 해요. 이렇게 근무를 하는 것에는 두 가지 장점이 있습니다. 우선 매일 출근을 하지 않아도 되죠. 이는 나이 든 사람들이 너무 지쳐 일을 하지 못하게 되는 상황을 막아 줄 것입니다. 노년층은 젊은 사람들보다 에너지가 부족하다는 점을 기억하세요. 또한 시간제 근무를 하면 그들의 생각이 새로워질 것인데, 이는 그들이 업무에 지루함을 느끼지 않을 것이라는 점을 의미하죠.

또 다른 아이디어를 알려 드릴게요. 제가 알기로 젊은 여러분은 모두 자신이 모든 것을 다 알고 있다고 생각하겠지만 하지만 여러분의 경험은 50대나 60대의 경험에 비교해 보면 아무것도 아닙니다. 기업들은 나이 든 직원들이 가진 능력을 최대한 활용해야 해요. 예를 들어 기업들이 이러한 사람들에게, 동일한 작업을 계속 반복하게 하는 대신, 보다 다양한 업무를 맡길 수도 있어요. 그리고 기업들이 나이 든 직원들과 더 자주 상의를 할 수도 있습니다. 이러한 노력을 통해 그들은 자신이 필요하다고 느끼게 될 것이고, 아울러 기업에서 일했던 수년간의 경험을 활용하게 될 거예요.

Note Taking

1) get worn out
2) become bored
3) a wider range of duties
4) feel wanted

| Comparing the Points |

Early Retirement for Elderly Employees

Reading (Problems)	Listening (Solutions)
Employees at the same jobs for many years become burned out and also bored by doing the same tasks again and again.	It is recommended that companies hire elderly employees on a part-time basis to keep them from becoming too worn out and to keep them interested in their work.

Older employees believe that they accomplish less than younger employees and therefore feel they are burdens on their companies.	Companies need to utilize older employees' experiences by giving them various tasks and also by consulting them on a more regular basis.

| Paraphrasing & Summarizing |

A

1   Nowadays, it has come to companies' attention that a great number of their elderly employees are quitting their jobs before they reach retirement age.

2   A large number of older workers have remained employed by their companies and are made to do the same tasks for considerably long periods of time.

3   Doing the same jobs repeatedly makes older workers simply get tired of the monotony of their jobs.

4   Elderly employees are often measuring themselves against employees younger than they are.

5   The elderly have trouble keeping up with younger workers, which gives them the feeling that they are not as productive as these younger employees.

Summary

Companies have long wondered why many of their workers began retiring in their fifties as opposed to their sixties, and now they have a couple of reasons as to why. First, many elderly employees become bored after doing the same jobs day after day for very long periods of time. They simply quit because they cannot handle the boredom of their work. Second, elderly workers recognize that they are being outworked by younger employees, which causes their opinions of their value to the company to decline. Realizing they are not as productive as they could be and that they are weighing down their employers with their presence, they just quit their jobs.

B

1   Let me carry on with some examples as to how we fail to help the elderly reach their full potential as workers.

2   Lots of older people would consider working only a few hours a week.

3   By only working part time, the elderly would not tax their brains and could remain interested in their work.

4   Many people in their teens and twenties are arrogant know-it-alls, but their knowledge pales in comparison to those more than twice their age.

5   The effects of being consulted would be to make the older employees feel that they belong and also to make

use of the stores of knowledge that have built up by their long years or employment.

Summary

The professor believes that it is pointless for people in their fifties to retire and not work anymore, so she provides some suggestions to get people to stop retiring so early. She thinks that instead of working full time, elderly people should be allowed to work part time. This measure would keep the employees fresh and eager to do their jobs. In addition, companies should try to involve their elderly employees in more activities and ask them for their opinions on various things. This effort would give elderly workers the confidence they require and at the same time also help their companies by having them rely upon people with many years of experience.

| Synthesizing |

1   The author of the reading passage claims that elderly employees get exhausted when they keep doing the same jobs repeatedly, so the professor suggests having elderly employees work merely on a part-time basis.

2   The problem in the reading is that elderly employees are no longer challenged by their daily routines but are instead bored with them, so the professor suggests that part-time work would help keep their minds fresh while also keeping the employees interested in doing their jobs.

3   In the reading, the author suggests that older employees cannot work as much as younger employees, thus making them less productive; however, the professor suggests giving them a wider range of duties and not having them repeat tasks all the time.

4   The author of the reading passage mentions that older workers feel that they are burdens on their companies because they do not contribute much, so the professor mentions that companies could consult them on a more regular basis.

| Organization |

1   The reading passage mentions a couple of reasons as to why elderly employees are retiring in their fifties before they are required to do so.

2   The professor provides a couple of solutions for the problems that are mentioned in the reading passage.

3   The first problem the reading mentions is that employees often retire after getting burned out and bored from repeatedly doing the same work.

4   So the professor believes companies should allow elderly employees to work part time, which will preserve their interest in their jobs.

5 In addition, working part time will keep the elderly from being bored at work and will keep their minds fresh.

6 Another problem leading to early retirement is that elderly employees compare themselves with younger employees and notice that they do less work and are burdening their companies.

7 Therefore, the professor suggests that companies could give their elderly employees many different tasks to do.

8 Additionally, companies could consult elderly employees on a more regular basis and draw upon their many years of experience.

9 By doing so, companies could make their older employees feel as though they are contributing more.

10 In conclusion, while the reading passage mentions a couple of important problems, the professor provides two methods that should effectively neutralize these problems and enable the elderly to contribute to their employers while not obligating them to take early retirement.

Writing

Sample Response

  The reading passage mentions a couple of reasons as to why elderly employees are retiring in their fifties before they are required to do so. The professor provides a couple of solutions for the problems that are mentioned in the reading passage.

  The first problem the reading mentions is that employees often retire after getting burned out and bored from repeatedly doing the same work. So the professor believes companies should allow elderly employees to work part time, which will preserve their interest in their jobs. In addition, working part time will keep the elderly from being bored at work and will keep their minds fresh.

  Another problem leading to early retirement is that elderly employees compare themselves with younger employees and notice that they do less work and are burdening their companies. Therefore, the professor suggests that companies could give their elderly employees many different tasks to do. Additionally, companies could consult elderly employees on a more regular basis and draw upon their many years of experience. By doing so, companies could make their older employees feel as though they are contributing more.

  In conclusion, while the reading passage mentions a couple of important problems, the professor provides two methods that should effectively neutralize these problems and enable the elderly to contribute to their

employers while not obligating them to take early retirement.

해석

  읽기 지문은 나이 든 직원들이 정년이 되기 전 50대에 퇴직을 하는 두 가지 이유를 언급한다. 교수는 읽기 지문에서 언급된 문제에 대한 두 가지 해결 방안을 제시한다.

  읽기 지문에서 언급된 첫 번째 문제는 직원들이 동일한 업무를 반복하다 보니 번아웃을 겪고 지루함을 느껴서 퇴직을 하는 일이 잦다는 것이다. 따라서 교수는 기업이 나이 든 직원들에게 시간제 근무를 시키면 그들이 업무에 대한 흥미를 잃지 않을 것이라고 생각한다. 또한 나이 든 직원들이 시간제 근무를 하면 일에서 지루함을 느끼지 않을 것이고 마음이 새로워지게 될 것이다.

  조기 퇴직을 야기하는 또 다른 문제는 나이 든 직원들이 자신과 젊은 직원들을 비교해서 자신들이 일을 덜하고 회사에 짐이 된다고 생각하는 점이다. 따라서 교수는 기업이 나이 든 직원들에게 여러 가지 다양한 업무를 맡길 것을 제안한다. 뿐만 아니라 기업은 보다 자주 나이 든 직원들과 상의를 하면서 그들이 가진 수년 간의 경험을 활용할 수 있을 것이다. 그렇게 하면 기업들이 나이 든 직원들로 하여금 자신의 기여도가 더 크다고 생각하도록 만들 수 있을 것이다.

  결론적으로 읽기 지문은 중요한 두 가지 문제를 언급하는 반면 교수는 이러한 문제를 효과적으로 해결하고 나이 든 직원들이 조기 퇴직을 강요받지 않으면서 고용주들에게 도움이 될 수 있는 두 가지 방안을 제안한다.

Unit 07 Education II

Exercise p.62

Reading

해석

  요즘 많은 대학들이 등록금을 인상하고 있다. 일부 경우에는 등록금 인상폭이 상당히 크다. 많은 학생들이 이러한 인상에 불만을 갖고 있지만 급격한 인상을 할 수밖에 없는 몇 가지 합리적인 이유가 존재한다.

  첫째, 대학은 교육의 질을 업그레이드하기 위해 끊임없이 노력한다. 요즘에는 대학을 다니는 사람의 수가 줄고 있기 때문에 학교측은 더 많은 학생을 유치하기 위해 분투해야 한다. 학생들을 끌어들일 수 있는 한 가지 이상적인 방법은 훌륭한 교육을 제공하는 것이다. 또한 학교의 학문적 위상을 높이면 학교측은 보다 많은 학생과 보다 우수한 학생을 유치하게 될 것이다. 교육의 질을 높이기 위해서는 비용을 지불해야 하기 때문에 학교 예산이 증가해야만 한다. 그러므로 등록금 또한 인상되어야 한다.

  둘째, 요즘 많은 대학들이 자금 부족 문제를 겪고 있다. 이는 특히 주립대의 경우에 심한데, 주립대는 종종 대학 예산의 대부분을 주에 의존하고 있다. 하지만 안타깝게도 많은 주들이 학교에 대한 지원금을 삭감하고 있다. 가장 큰 타격을 받는 부분은 대학의 일반 행정을 위한 지원금이다. 반드시 매력적인 일이라고 할 수는 없지만 일반 행정은 대학 복지에 매우 중요하다. 일반 행정을 위한 충분한 자금이 없으면 많은 학교들이 심각한 문제에 직면할 것이기 때문에 학교들은 다른 방법으로 줄어든 자금을 보충해야 한다. 따라서 바로 그러한 이유 때문에 학교들이 매년 등록금을 인상하는 것이다.

| Listening |

Script 🎧 01-08

M Professor: I'm sure many of you just got your tuition bills, and I know that most of you weren't pleased. Tuition went up by five percent this year for the fifth year in a row. Running a college is getting to be too expensive, but there are a few ways to offset this without raising your fees.

Everyone wants to improve our school's quality. But, you know, money isn't totally necessary to do this. For example, we should be looking at ourselves to improve our school. Take professors, for example. We could augment the quality of our lectures as well as develop better curriculums. And you, the students, could perform better both at school and after graduation. That would help increase our school's ranking without us spending much money or raising tuition.

Here's another idea, especially for engineering or science-heavy schools like ours. We should seek close ties with corporations. Why should we do this? Well, both of us will benefit. First, we'll get free state-of-the-art facilities, which both students and faculty will be able to use. Second, the corporations will get the inside track on recruiting our students to work for them once they graduate. And the corporations will know the students got an excellent education because they helped contribute to it. It's a win-win situation for both parties.

해석

M Professor: 분명 여러분 가운데 다수는 얼마 전에 등록금 고지서를 받고서 불만을 갖게 되었을 것으로 생각해요. 등록금은 5년 연속으로 5%씩 올랐습니다. 대학을 운영하는 일에 점점 더 많은 비용이 들고 있지만 등록금을 인상하지 않고 이를 해결할 수 있는 몇 가지 방법이 존재합니다.

모두가 학교의 질이 향상되기를 바랍니다. 하지만, 알다시피, 이렇게 하는데 전적으로 돈이 필요한 것은 아니에요. 예를 들어 학교를 발전시키기 위해 스스로를 살펴볼 수도 있습니다. 교수들을 예로 들어보죠. 우리는 강의의 질을 높일 수 있고 또한 더 나은 교과 과정을 개발할 수도 있을 거예요. 그리고 학생인 여러분들은 재학 중에, 그리고 졸업 후에 더 좋은 성과를 낼 수도 있을 것이고요. 그러면 많은 돈을 쓰거나 등록금을 인상하지 않고서도 학교의 위상을 높일 수 있습니다.

또 다른 아이디어가, 우리 대학처럼 공학이나 과학 분야가 특화된 학교를 위한, 아이디어가 있습니다. 우리는 기업과 긴밀한 관계를 맺을 수 있어요. 왜 그래야 할까요? 음, 양쪽 모두에게 도움이 될 것이기 때문입니다. 첫째, 우리는 무료로 최신 설비를 이용할 수 있는데, 학생과 교수진 모두가 이용을 할 수 있을 거예요. 그리고 둘째, 기업은 학생들이 졸업을 하면 학생들을 고용하는데 유리한 위치에 서게 됩니다. 그리고 기업은 학생들이 훌륭한 교육을 받았다는 점을 알 수 있는데, 그 이유는 그들이 교육에 기여를 했기 때문이죠. 양쪽 모두에게 도움이 되는 일입니다.

| Comparing the Points |

University Tuition Increases

Reading (Problems)	Listening (Solutions)
Schools need more money to improve the quality of education and to increase the school's academic ranking if they want to attract more and better students.	In order to improve the school, professors can improve curriculums and lectures while students can do better both in the classroom and after graduation.
Schools are getting their general budgets cut as well as seeing less funding go to their general management, so they have to make up for this loss with higher tuition.	Schools should increase their ties with corporations so that they may receive exceptional free facilities while the corporations will be able to recruit the students who learned with those facilities.

| Paraphrasing & Summarizing |

A

1 The large raises in tuition upset a lot of students even though schools have some good reasons for increasing the price of school.

2 Schools have to be more competitive in recruiting new students since not as many students are going to school as there used to be.

3 Good students will be more interested in attending a school that has a high academic ranking.

4 Because states are contributing less money to universities, the schools need to raise the necessary money by using other methods.

5 The department that runs the school is fairly unremarkable, but without it, the school would encounter many problems.

✔ Summary

Even though students at universities are not pleased about tuition increases, the schools have some good reasons for doing so. First, they have to improve themselves academically to attract more students, especially since fewer students are going to college nowadays. This requires money. So does raising the school's academic ranking, which will, in turn, attract better students to the school. A lot of schools also receive funding from various states. However, they are receiving less funding nowadays. Finally, the general management departments at these schools need enough money to run properly, or else the school will suffer. The schools therefore need to raise tuition to get more money.

B

1   Even though maintaining a school costs more every year, schools can still manage not to increase the price of tuition.

2   The members of the school body, including both students and faculty, should be able to make the school better by their own actions.

3   An inexpensive way to improve the school that does not require a tuition hike is for the students themselves to do better.

4   The schools will be able to receive outstanding new facilities that can be accessed by everyone attending and working at the school.

5   Since the companies were somewhat responsible for the students' educations, they will be aware of the high quality of education that the students have received.

✍ Summary

It actually is possible for universities to increase the quality of education that they offer without having to raise students' tuition. First, both the faculty and the students can improve themselves. The faculty can teach and prepare for classes better, and the students can improve their performance as well. These actions should increase the school's academic ranking without a need for a tuition hike. Schools should also strike agreements with corporations. The corporations can provide the schools with excellent free facilities. The schools will, in turn, produce well-educated students that the companies will then be able to recruit much more easily. This will also help schools avoid raising the cost of tuition.

| Synthesizing |

1   The reading passage mentions that universities can attract students by giving them an excellent education, so the professor responds by claiming that professors can improve the quality of their lectures while also preparing for class better.

2   The writer claims that an improvement in the school's academic ranking will cause more and better students to attend, which leads the professor to declare that the students can do a better job when attending school and

after graduating.

3   In response to the reading passage author's claim that cuts in the general funding of schools makes them have to look for funds elsewhere, the professor responds by saying that schools should make closer ties with corporations.

4   The writer claims that general management funds are disappearing, so the professor states that schools could get state-of-the-art facilities for free from various companies.

| Organization |

1   The professor states that schools do not have to raise tuition to improve the quality of education they provide for their students.

2   He then gives a couple of explanations as to how they can do this.

3   First, responding to the claim that schools need money to improve their academic ranking, the professor claims that the professors can do a better job of teaching and preparing for class.

4   He also mentions that the students can affect the school's academic rating in a positive manner.

5   They can study harder and get better jobs.

6   With a higher academic rating, the school will then be able to attract better students without having to raise tuition at all.

7   In addition, since schools are seeing their budgets cut by the state, the professor urges closer ties to businesses.

8   He claims the businesses can supply free facilities for the students to use.

9   These facilities will also offset budget losses to the university's general management funds.

10 The companies will also benefit by getting to hire competent workers when the students graduate.

11 If a school follows the professor's suggestions, he believes it will not have to increase tuition.

| Writing |

The professor states that schools do not have to raise tuition to improve the quality of education they provide for their students. He then gives a couple of explanations as to how they can do this.

First, responding to the claim that schools need money to improve their academic ranking, the professor claims that the professors can do a better job of teaching and preparing for class. He also mentions that the students can affect the school's academic rating in a positive manner. They can study harder and get better jobs. With a higher academic rating, the school will then be able to attract better students without having to raise tuition at all.

In addition, since schools are seeing their budgets cut by the state, the professor urges closer ties to businesses. He claims the businesses can supply free facilities for the students to use. These facilities will also offset budget losses to the university's general management funds. The companies will also benefit by getting to hire competent workers when the students graduate.

If a school follows the professor's suggestions, he believes it will not have to increase tuition.

해석

교수는 학교측이 학생들에게 제공하는 교육의 질을 향상시키기 위해 등록금을 인상할 필요가 없다고 말한다. 그런 다음 어떻게 그럴 수 있는지에 대한 두 가지 설명을 제시한다.

우선, 학교의 순위를 높이기 위해서는 학교에 돈이 필요하다는 주장에 대해 교수는 교수들이 강의와 수업 준비를 더 잘할 수 있다고 말한다. 그는 또한 학생들도 긍정적인 방법으로 학교의 학문적 평가에 영향을 미칠 수 있다고 말한다. 학생들은 공부도 더 열심히 하고 더 나은 직장을 구할 수 있다. 학문적 위상이 높아지면 학교는 등록금을 인상시키지 않고서도 보다 우수한 학생들을 유치할 수 있을 것이다.

또한, 학교들이 주로부터 받는 예산이 삭감되고 있기 때문에 교수는 기업들과 긴밀한 관계를 맺어야 한다고 주장한다. 그는 학생들이 사용할 수 있는 무료 시설을 기업들이 제공해 줄 수 있다고 주장한다. 이러한 시설은 학교의 일반 행정 기금에 대한 예산 삭감의 효과를 상쇄시켜 줄 것이다. 기업 역시 이러한 학생이 졸업을 하면 유능한 직원을 채용할 수 있기 때문에 혜택을 받는다.

학교측이 교수의 제안을 따른다면 교수는 등록금을 인상할 필요가 없을 것이라고 생각한다.

Unit 08 Environmental Science III

Exercise ·· p.70

| Reading |

해석

침입종은 지역 생태계에서 일어나는 대부분의 가장 심각한 문제들의 원인이다. 특히 먹이 사슬의 꼭대기에 새로운 종이 나타나면 생태계가 파괴되고 수많은 종들이 멸종할 수 있다. 미국의 수로에서 가장 많은 문제를 일으키고 있는 종은 얼룩무늬 홍합이다.

러시아 자생종인 얼룩무늬 홍합이 오대호 및 미국의 기타 여러 호수들과 강에 유입되었다. 얼룩무늬 홍합은 종종 선박의 바닥에 몸을 붙이는데, 이는 쉽게 이동을 할 수 있는 편리한 방법이다. 또한 이들은 때때로 송수관에 몸을 붙이기도 한다. 그 결과 관을 막히게 만들며 그러한 관 중 일부는 도시로 식수를 운반하는 데 사용되는 것이다. 시들이 막힌 관을 다시 뚫기 위해서는 막대한 비용이 든다. 또한 얼룩무늬 홍합은 매우 빠르게 번식하기 때문에 종종 다양한 물고기들과 다른 홍합들의 산란 장소를 완전히 덮어 버려서 그들의 성장을 방해한다.

둘째, 북미 지역의 얼룩무늬 홍합은 천적이 거의 없는데, 이는 이들이 강이나 호수에 자리를 잡으면 제거하기가 어렵다는 점을 의미한다. 게다가 과학자들은 얼룩무늬 홍합을 죽일 수 있는 환경친화적인 방법을 아직 찾지 못했다. 이러한 두 가지 사실 때문에 얼룩무늬 홍합은 극도로 빠르게 확산되고 있다. 만약 이러한 확산을 막지 못한다면 얼룩무늬 홍합이 곧 미국 전역의 수로에서 문제를 일으키게 될 것이다.

✎ Note Taking

1) Clog water pipes
2) Reproduce very rapidly
3) natural enemies
4) environmentally safe way

| Listening |

Script 🎧 01-09

W Professor: Yes, the zebra mussel is one of the worst invasive species to hit the United States. Scientists estimate it has cost billions of dollars in damages. While it's causing problems, there are a couple of methods that could help mitigate the damage it's causing. Let me explain.

One, everyone knows zebra mussels moved from Russia to America by traveling on boats. Well, there must be better decontamination procedures implemented to kill any mussels found hitchhiking on boats. Before a boat enters a lake or a river system, the ship's ballast should be sterilized with seawater, which kills the mussels. And the entire ship needs to be checked. Zebra mussels can survive out of water for several days, so the anchor chains and other parts out of water need to be decontaminated as well.

Two, there are some species of birds and fish that eat zebra mussels. For example, some ducks feed on them. Likewise, croakers, carp, and sturgeon are their natural predators. These species should be introduced to the waterways. Unfortunately, there are not enough of these birds and fish to have an impact on the mussels' numbers. Researchers must discover a way quickly to increase the numbers of these species in the hope that they will start to make a dent in the number of mussels. This effort will help control their expansion.

해석

W Professor: 네, 얼룩무늬 홍합은 미국에 피해를 입힌 최악의 침입종 중 하나입니다. 과학자들은 얼룩무늬 홍합이 수십 억 달러의 피해를 일으켰다고 추정하고 있어요. 얼룩무늬 홍합이 문제를 일으키고는 있지만 그로 인한 피해를 완화시킬 수 있는 두 가지 방법이 존재합니다.

첫째, 얼룩무늬 홍합이 선박을 타고 러시아에서 미국으로 이동했다는 점은 모두가 알고 있습니다. 음, 선박에 무임승차를 한 얼룩무늬 홍합을 모두 없애기 위해 사용할 수 있는 더 나은 제염법이 분명 있을 거예요. 선박이 호수나 강으로 진입하기 전에 선박의 밸러스트를 해수로 소독하면 얼룩무늬 홍합이 죽게 됩니다. 그리고 선박 전체를 확인해야 해요. 얼룩무늬 홍합은 물 밖에서도 며칠씩 생존할 수 있기 때문에 닻줄이나 물 밖에 드러나 있는 다른 부분들도 제독을 해야 합니다.

둘째, 얼룩무늬 홍합을 잡아먹는 조류와 어류가 있습니다. 예를 들어 몇몇 오리들은 얼룩무늬 홍합을 잡아먹어요. 마찬가지로 동갈민어, 잉어, 그리고 철갑상어 역시 얼룩무늬 홍합의 천적입니다. 이러한 종들을 수로에 유입시켜야 하죠. 안타까운 것은 이러한 조류와 어류가 얼룩무늬 홍합의 수에 영향을 미칠 만큼 많지는 않다는 점입니다. 연구자들은 이 종들이 얼룩무늬 홍합의 수를 감소시키기 시작할 것이라는 희망을 가지고 이러한 종의 수를 빠르게 증가시킬 수 있는 방법을 찾아야만 해요. 이러한 노력이 얼룩무늬 홍합의 확산을 억제하는데 도움이 될 것입니다.

✎Note Taking

1) Sterilize ships' ballasts
2) survive out of water
3) birds and fish
4) reduce the number of mussels

| Comparing the Points |

Zebra Mussels

Reading (Problems)	Listening (Solutions)
Zebra mussels have invaded America's waterways, where they clog water pipes and smother the spawning grounds of various fish and other mussels.	Before entering a waterway, ships' crews should sterilize their ballasts with salt water, and they must check the entire ship since mussels can survive out of water for days.
The zebra mussels have few natural enemies, and there are no environmentally safe methods to kill them, so scientists have not been able to reduce their numbers.	There are birds and fish that eat the mussels, so scientists must introduce them to the area and get their numbers to grow quickly so that they can start reducing the mussel population.

| Paraphrasing & Summarizing |

A

1   When a top predator appears in a new environment, it can wreak havoc on an ecosystem and completely wipe out many species.
2   While it comes from Russia, the zebra mussel now lives in American waterways like the Great Lakes.
3   Since zebra mussels have a high rate of reproduction, they can overrun the spawning grounds of other species, which keeps these species from growing larger in number.
4   In North America, the zebra mussel does not have many predators, which makes it difficult to find a natural solution to remove them from waterways.

5   If zebra mussels continue to expand their territories, all of America's lakes and river systems will have problems with them.

✓ Summary

When an invasive species moves into a new environment, it often causes problems for some native species, even causing them to go extinct. This is the case for the zebra mussel. Coming from Russia, the mussel rode on boats to get to America. There, it clogs pipes, which are expensive to unblock. It also reproduces so rapidly that it covers up the spawning grounds of other species, making these species reproduce more slowly. It is difficult to remove the mussels because they have few natural predators in North America. In addition, there is no environmentally safe way to kill them. If the mussels are not killed, they will soon expand to all of America's waterways.

B

1   There are some ways to solve the problems the zebra mussel is causing.
2   The crew needs to sterilize the ship's ballast with salt water to kill the mussels prior to entering any waterway.
3   Zebra mussels do not always live in the water, so crews need to search for them in every part of the ship that has touched water in order to eliminate them all.
4   Some animals and fish hunt zebra mussels.
5   If scientists can get predators of the zebra mussel to reproduce quickly, these animals will be able to reduce the number of mussels.

✓ Summary

While the zebra mussel has caused extremely expensive amounts of damage to America's waterways, there are some ways to control their numbers. First, crew members on ships can do a couple of things. They can fill the ship's ballast with seawater since that will kill them. They should also check the entire ship for mussels because they can survive out of water for a few days. In addition, there are some predators that prey upon the zebra mussels. These should be introduced to the waterways. Finally, since there are not enough of these predators, people need to make sure they reproduce rapidly. These solutions can then reduce the number of zebra mussels.

| Synthesizing |

1   The reading passage author writes that the mussels can travel easily since they attach themselves to the bottoms of boats, so the professor responds by arguing that the ship's ballast should be filled with seawater to kill them.

2 According to the professor, the entire boat should be decontaminated, even the parts out of water, so that the mussels will not be able to survive and harm the spawning grounds of other species, just like the reading passage describes.

3 As a response to the reading passage claim that there are few natural predators in North America which can remove zebra mussels, the professor mentions that people should introduce some of the zebra mussel's natural predators to the waterways.

4 Because there is no environmentally safe way to kill zebra mussels, the professor declares that researchers need to increase the number of predators so that these animals can start reducing the number of zebra mussels.

▌Organization▐

1 The professor talks about different ways to reduce the number of zebra mussels from America's waterways.

2 This is an invasive species from Russia that is causing many problems in America's rivers.

3 The professor provides a couple of solutions to this infestation problem.

4 First, she notes that all ships entering waterways should be sterilized with seawater, which kills the mussels.

5 She mentions this because mussels often hitch rides on the bottoms of ships.

6 The professor also notes that the mussels can survive out of water for days, so crew members should sterilize the entire ship.

7 This will keep the mussels from getting into the waterways and clogging up all the pipes.

8 Second, the professor states that some bird and fish species prey on the zebra mussel.

9 While the reading claims that it has few natural predators, the professor argues that they could be introduced.

10 She also thinks scientists should try to increase the numbers of these predators so that they can eat more mussels.

11 This will be beneficial because scientists know of no environmentally safe way to kill the mussels.

12 Although the zebra mussel is causing many problems, the professor seems confident that her ideas will help eliminate them.

▌Writing▐

Sample Response

The professor talks about different ways to reduce the number of zebra mussels from America's waterways. This is an invasive species from Russia

that is causing many problems in America's rivers. The professor provides a couple of solutions to this infestation problem.

First, she notes that all ships entering waterways should be sterilized with seawater, which kills the mussels. She mentions this because mussels often hitch rides on the bottoms of ships. The professor also notes that the mussels can survive out of water for days, so crew members should sterilize the entire ship. This will keep the mussels from getting into the waterways and clogging up all the pipes.

Second, the professor states that some bird and fish species prey on the zebra mussel. While the reading claims that it has few natural predators, the professor argues that they could be introduced. She also thinks scientists should try to increase the numbers of these predators so that they can eat more mussels. This will be beneficial because scientists know of no environmentally safe way to kill the mussels.

Although the zebra mussel is causing many problems, the professor seems confident that her ideas will help eliminate them.

해석

교수는 미국의 수로에서 얼룩무늬 홍합의 수를 줄일 수 있는 여러 가지 방법에 대해 이야기한다. 이 얼룩무늬 홍합은 러시아에서 온 침입종으로 미국의 강에 많은 문제를 야기하고 있다. 교수는 이러한 침입 문제에 대해 두 가지 해결 방안을 제시한다.

첫째, 그녀는 수로에 진입하는 모든 선박을 해수로 소독해 얼룩무늬 홍합을 제거해야 한다고 말한다. 그녀가 이렇게 말하는 이유는 얼룩무늬 홍합이 선박의 바닥에 붙어서 이동을 하기 때문이다. 또한 교수는 얼룩무늬 홍합이 물 밖에서도 며칠 동안 살 수 있기 때문에 선원들이 선박 전체를 소독해야 한다고 말한다. 그렇게 하면 얼룩무늬 홍합이 수로에 들어와 모든 관들을 막는 일을 예방하게 될 것이다.

둘째, 교수는 몇몇 조류와 어류가 얼룩무늬 홍합을 잡아먹는다고 주장한다. 읽기 지문에는 천적이 거의 없다고 나와 있지만 교수는 천적을 도입할 수 있을 것이라고 말한다. 또한 그녀는 과학자들이 이러한 천적이 더 많은 얼룩무늬홍합을 잡아먹을 수 있도록 천적의 수를 늘리기 위해 노력해야 한다고 생각한다. 과학자들이 얼룩무늬 홍합을 없앨 수 있는 환경친화적인 방법을 모르고 있기 때문에 그러한 방법이 도움이 될 것이다.

얼룩무늬 홍합이 많은 문제를 일으키고 있지만 교수는 자신의 아이디어가 이들을 제거하는데 도움이 될 것으로 확신하는 것처럼 보인다.

Unit 09 Education I

Exercise 1 .... p.84

| Brainstorming & Outlining |

A

Professor Cartwright

해석

다음 시간에는 온라인 학습에 대해 논의할 거예요. 모든 곳에서의 학습에 커다란 변화를 가져오고 있죠. 여기에는 대학 및 기타 교육 기관들도 포함됩니다. 토론 게시판에 있는, 모두가 생각해 보았으면 하는 질문을 알려 드릴게요. 여러분의 생각에는 온라인 학습의 가장 중요한 결과가 무엇인가요?

B

Jacqueline

해석

제 생각에는 전 세계 모든 사람들이 교육을 받을 수 있다는 것이 온라인 학습의 가장 중요한 결과입니다. 인터넷 덕분에 사람들은 교육을 받으러 더 이상 물리적인 학교에 다닐 필요가 없어요. 대신 집에서, 혹은 사실 그 밖의 어디에서라도, 온라인 학습을 활용할 수 있고 양질의 교육을 받을 수가 있습니다.

📝 Summary Notes: Jacqueline

1) attend physical school
2) at homes
3) anywhere else
4) quality education

Harold

해석

대부분의 온라인 수업은 대학 혹은 대학교에서의 비슷한 수업들보다 훨씬 수강료가 저렴해요. 따라서 개인의 경제적인 상황과 그 사람의 학습 능력은 더 이상 아무런 관계가 없게 되었습니다. 많은 사람들이 높은 등록금 때문에 대학에 다니지 못합니다. 하지만 저렴한 온라인 수업 때문에 더 이상 그런 경우는 없게 되었어요.

📝 Summary Notes: Harold

1) Financial status
2) learn more
3) no college
4) price of tuition
5) online classes

| Organization |

Supporting Jacqueline's Opinion

1 I like the answers that Jacqueline and Harold provide, but I believe something else is more important.

2 For me, the flexibility that online learning offers people is key.

3 Most online classes allow students to study at their own pace.

4 They can therefore finish a course in a week's time or take longer.

5 The only important thing is that students do the coursework and complete their assignments.

6 This benefits people with jobs a tremendous amount.

7 For instance, they may not have time to attend traditional classes, yet they can take online classes at night and on weekends.

8 This enables them to improve their knowledge while still keeping their jobs.

Supporting Harold's Opinion

1 The fact that people can take online classes from anywhere in the world is the most important result.

2 Not everyone is interested in going to another city or country to study.

3 They might not be able to afford it, or perhaps they have no interest in leaving their current place of residence.

4 Whatever the case, taking online classes does not require them to relocate.

5 This feature is also important to people with disabilities.

6 They may find it difficult—or even impossible—to attend physical classes.

7 But as long as they can view a computer monitor, they can study online.

8 To me, that is the most positive aspect of online classes.

Exercise 2 .... p.87

Professor Ward

해석

스마트폰은 지난 수십 년 동안 가장 큰 영향을 끼친 과학 기술 중 하나입니다. 전화 통화 및 문자 수신 외에도 수많은 기능을 가지고 있죠. 하지만 또한 사람들의, 특히 십대들의 집중력을 떨어뜨릴 수도 있습니다. 고등학교가 학생들이 학교에 스마트폰을 가져오는 것을 금지시켜야 한다고 생각하나요? 찬반인 이유는요?

Carter

해석

고등학교에서 학생들이 학교에 스마트폰을 가져오는 것은 반드시 금지되어야 해요. 수업 시간에 너무나 많은 학생들이 전화기를 갖고 노느라 선생님의 말씀을 무시합니다. 그 결과 학업에 태만해지는데, 이는 교육에 지장을 주고 그들의 장래에 해를 끼칩니다. 고등학교 학생들이 학교에 스마트폰을 가져올 이유가 전혀 없습니다.

Beatrice

해석

저는 고등학교 학생들이 학교에 스마트폰을 가져오는 것이 용인할 만한 일이라고 생각해요. 물론 수업 시간에는 집중력을 잃지 않도록 스마트폰 사용을 금지해야 하죠. 어쨌거나 스마트폰은 인터넷 접속을 가능하게 만들기 때문에 조사를 위한 도구로 활용될 수 있어요. 따라서 학생들은 그러한 기능을 이용해서 학습용으로 스마트폰을 사용할 수가 있습니다.

✏ Summary Notes

Carter

1) Students ignore teachers
2) Hinders education

Beatrice

1) Avoid distractions
2) Can access Internet

Sample Response 1 Supporting Carter

> While I understand both sides of the argument, I think Carter makes a strong point. So many students are addicted to their smartphones, which makes them use their phones at inappropriate times. This includes class, which is when students should be learning, not surfing the Internet or updating their social media pages. In addition, smartphones are expensive with some costing a thousand dollars or more. Students could lose or damage them at school. Bad students or bullies could steal their phones as well. This would cause students great financial loss. To avoid these problems, the best option would be for high schools to ban smartphone from the premises.

해석

양쪽 주장 모두 이해가 가지만 나는 Carter가 중요한 점을 지적하고 있다고 생각한다. 너무 많은 학생들이 스마트폰에 중독되어서 적절하지 못한 때에 전화기를 사용한다. 여기에는 수업도 포함되는데, 수업에서는 학생들이 인터넷 서핑이나 소셜 미디어 페이지를 업데이트해서는 안 되고 공부를 해야 한다. 또한 스마트폰은 가격이 매우 비싸며 일부 스마트폰은 1천 달러 이상의 가격이 나가기도 한다. 학생들은 학교에서 스마트폰을 분실하거나 파손시킬 수 있다. 또한 나쁜 학생들이나 불량 학생들이 전화기를 훔칠 수도 있다. 그러면 학생들이 막대한 금전적인 손해를 보게 될 것이다. 이러한 문제를 피하기 위한 최선의 방안은 고등학교가 학교에서 스마트폰을 금지시키는 것이다.

Sample Response 2 Supporting Beatrice

> I see the point that Carter is making, but Beatrice has the right idea. It is fine for students to bring smartphones to high school. Many students, myself included, use smartphones to conduct research. High school students should be able to go online between classes to help them complete school assignments such as homework and research projects. Another advantage of having smartphones at school is that students may need them in case of an emergency. Parents may need to contact their children immediately for various reasons. However, if smartphones are banned from campus, this cannot happen. High schools should allow smartphones but simply place restrictions on their usage.

해석

나는 Carter가 말하는 요점을 이해하지만 Beatrice의 아이디어가 옳다고 생각한다. 학생들이 고등학교에 스마트폰을 가지고 오는 것은 괜찮다. 나 자신을 포함하여 많은 학생들이 스마트폰을 이용해 조사를 한다. 고등학교 학생들은 수업 시간 사이에 온라인에 접속해서 숙제 및 조사 프로젝트와 같은 학교 과제들을 수행할 수 있다. 학교에 스마트폰을 가져오는 것의 또 다른 장점은 긴급한 상황에서 학생들이 이를 사용할 수 있다는 점이다. 여러 가지 이유로 부모들이 자녀들에게 즉시 연락해야 하는 경우가 있을 수 있다. 하지만 교내에서 스마트폰이 금지된다면 그럴 수 없을 것이다. 고등학교는 스마트폰을 허용하되 사용에만 제한을 두면 된다.

Unit 10 Sociology I

Exercise 1 .... p.90

‖ Brainstorming & Outlining ‖

A

Professor Hampton

해석

오늘날 전 세계 도시 중심지에서 인구가 증가하고 있습니다. 한 가지 결과는 이러한 도시들이 항상 교통 문제에 대처해야 한다는 것이에요. 여기에는 도로 혼잡과 몇 시간 동안 지속될 수 있는 교통 체증이 포함되죠. 도시가 교통 문제를 해결할 수 있는 최선의 방법은 무엇이라고 생각하나요? 왜 그렇게 생각하죠?

B

Madeline

해석

분명 교통 문제를 해결할 수 있는 최선의 방법은 대중 교통을 강조하는 것입니다. 도시는 버스 및 지하철 시스템을 강화하고 확대시켜야 해요. 버스와 지하철 노선이, 인근의 교외 지역을 포함해서, 충분히 많은 곳까지 확대되면 보다 많은 사람들이 운전을 하지 않게 될 거예요. 이로써 교통 체증이 줄어들 것이고 도로 혼잡도 완화될 것입니다.

✏ Summary Notes: Madeline

1) bus and subway systems
2) suburbs
3) quit driving
4) traffic jams
5) congestion

Leonard

해석

제 생각으로는 도시들이 많은 도로들을, 특히 수많은 차량들이 다니는 고가 도로를 넓혀야 합니다. 이들 도로를 넓힘으로써 자동차, 트럭, 그리고 기타 차량들이 다닐 수 있는 공간이 더 많아질 거예요. 그러면 교통 체증을 없애는데 도움이 될 것이고 통근자들은 평소보다 훨씬 더 빠르게 출퇴근을 하게 될 것입니다.

✍ Summary Notes: Leonard

1) many roads
2) elevated roads
3) more space
4) eliminate traffic jams
5) work and home

❚ Organization ❚

Supporting New Ideas: Banning Vehicles from Roads

1 Madeline and Leonard propose interesting solutions, but I believe in taking more serious action.

2 I suggest that cities should ban certain vehicles from the roads each day.

3 For instance, perhaps cars whose license plates end with an odd number cannot drive on Mondays, Wednesdays, and Fridays.

4 This would reduce the number of vehicles on city roads by half.

5 This has been done in some cities and has worked.

6 It would have the added benefit of forcing people to use public transportation.

7 Another benefit would be that pollution from vehicle emissions would be reduced, so the air would be cleaner.

8 My solution to urban traffic problems would have several advantages.

Supporting New Ideas: Carpooling in Cities

1 I like Madeline's and Leonard's responses, but I have a different idea.

2 A simple way to reduce traffic congestion would be to encourage carpooling.

3 Many cars on city roads have a single driver.

4 If people would carpool, three, four, or five people would ride together in a single car.

5 Those people's cars would be removed from the roads since they would no longer be driving.

6 Drivers would also save money since they would not have to put gas in their cars so often.

7 They could relax or do work while another person drives, too.

8 This simple solution could have multiple benefits for cities that encourage carpooling.

Exercise 2 ·· p.93

Professor Robinson
해석

예전에는 많은 가정에 3명, 4명, 혹은 5명의 아이들이 있었습니다. 하지만 최근 가구당 아이의 수가 줄고 있어요. 그 이유로는 경제적인 어려움과 인구 과잉에 대한 두려움을 들 수 있습니다. 하지만 한 국가의 인구가 안정적으로 유지되기 위해서는 출생률이 약 2가 되어야 합니다. 가정에 두세 명의 아이들이 있어야 한다고 생각하나요, 아니면 한 명이나 전혀 없어도 된다고 생각하나요? 그 이유는요?

Tyler
해석

아이들은 대단한 존재이기 때문에 저는 가정에 여러 명의 아이들이 있기를 바랍니다. 인간이 이주할 수 있는, 아직 사람이 살지 않는 곳이 엄청나게 많아서 세계는 사실 인구 과잉 상태가 아니에요. 아이들은 또한 미래이기 때문에 인류가 멸종하지 않기 위해서는 최대한 많은 아이들이 필요합니다.

Amanda
해석

사람들은 아이를 많이 낳는 이기적인 행동을 그만두어야 해요. 한 명의 아이를 갖거나 아이를 갖지 않은 것이 결혼한 부부의 목표가 되어야 합니다. 세상에는, 기아, 전쟁, 그리고 환경 문제를 포함해서, 너무 많은 문제들이 존재해요. 우리는 아이들이 고통을 겪고 힘든 삶을 살 가능성이 높은 세상으로 아이들을 데려와서는 안 됩니다.

✍ Summary Notes

Tyler

1) Humans can move to them
2) Need as many children as possible

Amanda

1) Hunger, wars, and environmental issues
2) Should not bring children into world where they will suffer

Sample Response 1 Supporting Tyler

I could not disagree with Amanda more. Tyler is correct in that we need families to have as many children as possible. First, as he mentions, the world is not overpopulated. There are places everywhere around the world, including on and under the oceans, where human dwellings could be built. I am not concerned about resources either. There are plenty of resources not only on the Earth but also in space. Thanks to developments in technology, asteroid mining will be possible soon. That will provide metals and other valuable resources for humans to use. It is totally fine and highly advisable for families to have multiple children.

해석

나는 Amanda의 의견에 전적으로 동의하지 않는다. 우리에게는 최대한 많은 아이가 있는 가정이 필요하다는 Tyler의 말이 옳다. 우선, 그가 언급한 것과 같이, 세상은 인구 과잉 상태가 아니다. 전 세계 모든 곳에서, 바다 위와 바다 아래를 포함하여, 인간의 거주지가 만들어질 수 있다. 또한 나는 자원 걱정도 하지 않는다. 지구뿐만 아니라 우주에도 많은 자원이 존재한다. 과학 기술의 발전으로 소행성 채굴도 곧 가능해질 것이다. 그러면 인간이 사용할 수 있는 금속 및 기타 귀중한 자원들이 공급될 것이다. 가정에 여러 명의 아이들이 있는 것은 전적으로 좋은 일이며 매우 바람직한 일이다.

The arguments made by Tyler and Amanda are compelling, but I side with Amanda. She is right in pointing out that the Earth has many problems. Personally, I plan to have no children unless progress is made in solving these problems. Something else to think about is that these days, most parents work. Because of that, children must spend time at daycare centers. It is not fair to children to make them spend so much time away from their parents. If parents cannot raise their children themselves, they should not have any children. That means families should have zero or one child at the most.

해석

Tyler와 Amanda가 제기한 주장은 설득력이 있지만 나는 Amanda와 생각이 같은 편이다. 지구에 많은 문제가 존재한다는 그녀의 지적은 옳다. 개인적으로 나는 이러한 문제들의 해결에 있어서 진전이 이루어지지 않는 한 아이를 가질 계획이 없다. 생각해야 할 또 다른 점은 오늘날 대부분의 부모들이 일을 한다는 것이다. 이 때문에 아이들은 보육 기관에서 시간을 보내야만 한다. 아이들이 부모와 떨어져 그처럼 많은 시간을 보내도록 만드는 것은 부당한 일이다. 부모가 직접 아이를 기를 수 없다면 아이를 가져서는 안 된다. 이는 가정에 아이가 없거나 최대 한 명의 아이가 있어야 한다는 점을 의미한다.

Unit 11 Economics

Exercise 1 ·· p.96

| Brainstorming & Outlining |

A

Professor Olsen

해석

다음 수업에서는 중소기업에 대해 논의할 예정입니다. 여러분들이 토론 게시판에 게시하기를 바라는 것을 말씀드릴게요. 사업을 시작하는 많은 사람들이 파트너를 찾습니다. 여러분의 생각으로 잠재적인 사업 파트너를 선택할 때 가장 중요한 기준은 무엇인가요? 왜 그렇게 생각하죠?

B

Diana

해석

사업 파트너의 굳건한 직업 윤리가 매우 중요합니다. 두 파트너 모두 열심히 일을 한다면 그 벤처 기업은 성공할 가능성이 높아요. 한 파트너의 직업 윤리가 약한 경우에는 사업이 실패할 것입니다. 또한 한 사람이 다른 사람보다 더 열심히 일할 것이기 때문에 파트너 사이에 갈등이 일어날 수도 있습니다.

✐ Summary Notes: Diana

1) Vital
2) hard

3) succeed
4) Poor
5) fail
6) Cause friction
7) harder

Bruce

해석

제가 찾는 것은 창의력입니다. 요즘에는 비슷한 기업들이 너무나 많아요. 창의력이 높은 파트너는 남들과 다른 새로운 사업을 할 수가 있을 것입니다. 이로써 고객과 투자가들의 관심을 끌게 될 것이고, 그렇게 되면 사업이 수익을 낼 가능성이 높아질 것입니다.

✐ Summary Notes: Bruce

1) similar businesses
2) different from others
3) customers and investors

| Organization |

Supporting New Ideas: Having Business Experience

1 While Diana and Bruce have thought of good criteria, I believe another factor is more important.
2 For me, business experience is key for a partner.
3 Many people have great ideas they want to monetize; however, they have no business experience.
4 This results in them not making money from their idea.
5 A partner with business experience would help a company in many ways.
6 For example, the person would know how to attract investors and how to promote the business.
7 The person would also know the ins and outs of running a business in general.
8 To me, that is easily the most necessary criterion in a business partner.

Supporting New Ideas: Being Honest

1 I like the ideas suggested by Diana and Bruce, yet I would look for something different.
2 In my view, honesty is the most important criterion in a business partner.
3 An honest person will not cheat his or her partner.
4 I have read about many business ventures that have failed because one partner was stealing from the firm.
5 That would not happen if the partner were honest.
6 In addition, an honest partner would tell the truth to investors and customers even if the truth is not positive.
7 That will make a good impression on them.
8 As a result, the chances of success will increase dramatically.

Professor Kimble

해석

요즘 광고 제작자들은 매우 영악합니다. 보통 자신의 제품이나 서비스를 구매할 가능성이 가장 높은 사람들을 대상으로 광고를 하죠. 하지만 일부 타깃 광고는 아이들을 그 대상으로 삼습니다. 몇몇 사람들은 이러한 광고가 아이들을 조종해서 불필요한 제품을 사도록 만든다고 생각하죠. 아이들을 대상으로 한 타깃 광고가 금지되어야 한다고 생각하나요? 찬반인 이유는요?

Julie

해석

광고 제작자들이 아이를 대상으로 삼는 것은 잘못된 일이기 때문에 저는 그러한 광고가 금지되어야 한다고 생각합니다. 아이들에게는 보통 스스로 쓸 수 있는 돈이 거의 없거나 아예 없어요. 그럼에도 불구하고 부모가 사 줄 때까지 애원하고 조를 수가 있죠. 그 결과 실제로는 필요하지 않은 제품에 가정들이 돈을 쓰게 됩니다.

Robert

해석

저는 광고 제작자들이 아이들을, 심지어 매우 어린 아이들을 대상으로 삼아도 아무런 문제가 없다고 생각합니다. 단지 부모들이 책임감을 가지고 아이들의 TV 시청을 감독하면 되는 것이죠. 게다가 부모들이 아이들에게 안 된다고 말해서 특정 제품을 구매하지 않을 수도 있어요. 부모가 엄격해야 하고 아이들의 요구에 굴복해서는 안 됩니다.

✎ Summary Notes

Julie

1) Beg parents to make purchases
2) Families waste money on items don't need

Robert

1) Parents should be responsible
2) Don't give in to children's desires

Sample Response 1 Supporting Julie

I understand the point Robert is making, but I agree with Julie. Targeted advertising for children has the potential to be extremely harmful. As Julie mentions, children often attempt to persuade their parents to make purchases. This can harm low-income families and make parents angry at their children. This often results in unhappy families. Another thing is that many parents work, so children are frequently home alone. If they watch TV, they see targeted ads constantly. This can cause harm to the children, who get convinced they need certain items. For those reasons, I strongly oppose targeted ads for children and hope they are banned.

해석

나는 Robert의 주장을 이해하지만 Julie의 의견에 동의한다. 아이들을 대상으로 하는 타깃 광고는 잠재적으로 매우 위험하다. Julie가 언급한 것처럼 아이들은 종종 부모를 설득해서 물건을 구입한다. 이는 저소득층 가정에게 피해를 줄 수 있고 부모가 아이들에게 화를 내도록 만들 수 있다. 그 결과 종종 가정이 불행

해진다. 또 다른 점은 많은 부모가 일을 하기 때문에 아이들이 집에 혼자 있는 경우가 많다는 것이다. 아이들이 TV를 시청하면 항상 타깃 광고를 보게 된다. 이로 인해 아이들에게 피해가 갈 수 있는데, 아이들은 특정 제품이 필요하다는 설득을 당하게 된다. 이러한 이유들로 나는 아이들을 대상으로 삼는 타깃 광고를 반대하며 그러한 광고가 금지되기를 바란다.

Sample Response 2 Supporting Robert

While Julie makes a good argument, Robert has the right idea. There is no need to prohibit targeted advertising for children. Robert is correct in stating that parents can say no to their children. Parents must remember that they, not their children, are in charge. Parents can also take the opportunity to instruct their children about targeted ads. Parents can point out how advertising agencies are trying to manipulate them. Parents should seize the chance to show their children how to resist these ads. They can provide a lesson on self-control and not impulsively making purchases. I therefore see no need to ban targeted ads for children.

해석

Julie도 적절한 주장을 하고 있지만 Robert의 생각이 맞다. 아이들을 대상으로 하는 타깃 광고를 금지할 필요는 없다. 부모들이 아이들에게 안 된다고 말할 수 있다는 Robert의 말이 옳다. 부모는 자신에게, 아이가 아니라, 책임이 있다는 점을 기억해야 한다. 부모는 또한 타깃 광고에 대해 아이들을 가르칠 수 있는 기회를 가질 수 있다. 광고 회사들이 아이들을 어떻게 조종하려고 하는지 알려 줄 수 있다. 부모들은 기회를 잡아서 아이들에게 어떻게 그런 광고에 대응해야 하는지 알려 주어야 한다. 자제력을 기르고 충동 구매를 하지 않도록 교육할 수 있다. 따라서 아이들을 대상으로 하는 타깃 광고를 금지할 필요는 없는 것으로 보인다.

Unit **12** Environmental Science

❙ Brainstorming & Outlining ❙

A

Professor Thompson

해석

오늘날 수많은 사람들이 개인 차량을 소유하고 있고 비행기로 이동을 합니다. 하지만 이러한 운송 수단들은 또한 해로운 배기 가스를 대기로 방출시키는 원인이기도 해요. 이로 인해 대기 오염 및 기타 문제들이 발생하고 있습니다. 생각해 보세요. 사람들은 자동차나 비행기로 이동을 할 때마다 이들이 일으키는 오염 때문에 이용료를 부과해야 합니다. 이에 동의하나요, 아니면 반대하나요? 그 이유는요?

B

Orville

해석

대기 오염은 많은 부정적인 영향을 미치며 자동차와 비행기는 대기 오염의 주범

입니다. 따라서 저는 그러한 주장에 동의해요. 차량 운전 및 비행기 이용에 대한 요금을 부과하면 국가들이 대기 오염과 맞설 수 있는 기금이 마련될 것입니다. 따라서 사람들은 자신이 일으키는 문제를 해결하기 위해 비용을 내는 셈이죠. 저는 그것이 공정하다고 생각합니다.

✍ Summary Notes: Orville

1) negative effects
2) primary contributors
3) air pollution
4) funds
5) problems they cause
6) Fair

Mae
해석

저는 그러한 주장을 전적으로 반대합니다. 우리나라의 수백만 명의 사람들이 수십 년 동안 운전을 하고 비행기를 이용해 왔어요. 그런 기본적인 권리에 갑자기 요금을 부과하는 것은 잘못된 일입니다. 이는 기본적으로 세금에 해당될 것인데, 정부는 사람들로부터 이미 충분한 세금을 걷고 있어요. 사람들은 이동할 권리를 가지고 있으며, 이동을 하기 위해 요금을 지불할 필요는 없습니다.

✍ Summary Notes: Mae

1) decades
2) charge fee
3) tax
4) Government taxes
5) right to travel
6) pay

‖ Organization ‖

Supporting Orville's Opinion

1 While this topic is controversial, I agree with Orville and support assessing a fee for driving and flying.
2 Orville correctly notes that the funds raised could be used to clean up the air.
3 Since drivers and flyers are responsible for the air pollution, it is logical to charge them for the solution.
4 Something else is that paying a fee would make some people cease driving or flying.
5 This would result in emissions reductions, so the Earth's atmosphere would become less polluted.
6 We must think about other people and future generations.
7 We should do everything possible to provide them with a clean and healthy planet.
8 I therefore support the statement.

Supporting Mae's Opinion

1 Although it is true that cars and planes contribute to air pollution, I do not agree that people should pay a fee.

2 As Mae remarks, it would be a tax on driving and flying.
3 People should not be taxed on something they have a right to do.
4 Let me add that many people are suffering financial difficulties nowadays and cannot afford to pay a fee.
5 For drivers, this would be incredibly harmful.
6 Some people would give up driving and then have no way to get to their jobs and to run errands.
7 Although air pollution is a problem, charging a driving and flying fee is not the solution.

Exercise 2 ⋯⋯⋯⋯⋯⋯⋯⋯⋯⋯⋯⋯⋯⋯⋯⋯⋯⋯⋯⋯⋯⋯⋯ p.105

Professor Jackson
해석
다음 수업에서는 어떻게 인간이 다양한 종을 멸종 위기에 몰아넣고 이들을 멸종시켰는지에 대해 논의할 것입니다. 토론 게시판에 있는, 여러분이 생각해 보아야 할 질문을 알려 드릴게요. 인간이 멸종 위기종을 보호하기 위해 조치를 취하고 그들의 수가 유지되거나 증가하도록 만들어야 할까요? 찬반인 이유는요?

Leia
해석
우리 인간이 도도새와 같은 종들을 멸종시키고 모든 대륙에 살고 있는 종의 수를 감소하게 만들었다는 점은 부끄럽게 생각해요. 우리는 반드시 멸종 위기종을 보호하기 위한 조치를 취해야 합니다. 간단한 방법은 동물이 어떤 식으로든 사냥을 당하거나 해를 입을 것이라는 걱정을 하지 않고 살아갈 수 있는 자연 보호 구역을 더 많이 만드는 것이에요.

Brandon
해석
저는 우리가 멸종 위기종을 보호하기 위해 조치를 취해야 한다고 생각하지 않습니다. 우선 전 세계에는 인간이 거주하지 않는 지역이 있는데, 이곳에서는 동물들이 평화롭게 살 수 있고 어디에서도 인간의 모습을 볼 수 없을 거예요. 또한 지구 역사를 통틀어 종들은 멸종해 왔습니다. 어떤 종이 지구의 상황에 적응을 하지 못하면 멸종하게 놔두어야 해요.

✍ Summary Notes

Leia

1) Have reduced animals' numbers everywhere
2) Establish nature preserves

Brandon

1) No humans in sight
2) Species have gone extinct throughout history

Sample Response 1 Supporting Leia

There should be nothing controversial about this statement. We humans should be stewards of the Earth, which means we must protect endangered species. I support Leia's suggestion of creating more nature preserves for animals. I would go even further and make harsh penalties for people caught harming animals in them. We should also move animal populations to places where they could thrive. For instance, if humans are encroaching on a certain animal's territory, we could move the animals to a new habitat. This would let the animals survive while also allowing humans to develop land. Through these two methods, we could protect endangered species and help them increase their populations.

해석

그러한 주장에는 논란의 여지가 없다. 우리 인간은 지구의 집사여야 하는데, 이는 우리가 멸종 위기종을 보호해야 한다는 점을 의미한다. 나는 동물들을 위해 더 많은 자연 보호 구역을 만들어야 한다는 Leia의 주장을 지지한다. 나는 더 나아가 보호 구역 내에서 동물들에게 해를 끼치다 붙잡힌 사람들을 가혹하게 처벌하는 것을 원한다. 또한 동물들이 번성할 수 있는 곳으로 동물 무리를 이동시켜야 한다. 예를 들어 인간이 특정 동물의 영역을 침범하는 경우, 우리는 그 동물을 새로운 서식지로 옮겨다 놓을 수 있을 것이다. 그러면 동물들이 번성하게 되고 또한 인간은 토지를 개발할 수 있을 것이다. 이러한 두 가지 방법을 통해 우리는 멸종 위기종을 보호하고 그들의 개체수를 증가시킬 수 있다.

Sample Response 2 Supporting Brandon

Similar to Brandon, I oppose doing anything to help endangered species. He makes a great point that animals have gone extinct for millions of years. When a species' time on the Earth is done, we should let it go extinct. A new species will appear and replace it. We should also put the needs of humans ahead of animals. In some places, misguided governments ban progress to protect unimportant animals. For example, dams have been knocked down on behalf of tiny fish. This harms humans, who used to get electricity from those dams. While we should not actively eliminate endangered species, we do not need to protect them.

해석

Brandon과 마찬가지로 나는 멸종 위기종을 돕기 위해 무언가를 하는 것을 반대한다. 그는 동물들이 수백만 년 동안 멸종해 왔다는 적절한 지적을 하고 있다. 지구에서 어떤 종의 시대가 끝나면 우리는 그 종이 멸종하게 놔두어야 한다. 새로운 종이 나타나서 그 종을 대체하게 될 것이다. 우리는 또한 동물보다 인간의 필요를 우선시해야 한다. 어떤 곳에서는 잘못 판단한 정부가 중요하지도 않은 동물을 보호하기 위해 발전을 막고 있다. 예를 들어 작은 물고기들을 위해 댐이 허물어지고 있다. 이는 댐에서 전기를 얻었던 인간에게 해가 되는 일이다. 우리가 멸종 위기종을 적극적으로 멸종시켜서는 안 되겠지만 그들을 보호할 필요는 없다.

Unit **13** **Education II**

Exercise 1 .... p.108

Brainstorming & Outlining

A

Professor Jefferson
해석

내일 수업에서는 다양한 교수법을 다룰 예정입니다. 수업 전에 여러분이 생각해 보았으면 하는 것을 알려 드리죠. 일부 교수들은 전체 수업 시간 동안 주로 강의를 함으로써 수업을 진행해요. 수업에서 학생들의 참여를 요구하는, 전형적으로는 토론 수업을 자주 하는 교수들도 있습니다. 여러분은 어떤 유형의 수업을 선호하나요? 그 이유는요?

B

Rudolph
해석

교수가 강의만 하는 수업이 제가 선호하는 방식입니다. 어쨌거나 교수는 해당 분야의 전문가이기 때문에 저는 수업 시간 내내 강의를 하는 교수의 수업을 들음으로써 본전을 찾고자 합니다. 학생들의 의견이 듣고 싶으면 수업이 끝난 직후에 급우들과 이야기를 나누면 되죠.

✎ Summary Notes: Rudolph

1) experts in fields
2) money's worth
3) entire class
4) after class

Angelina
해석

저는 사실 토론이 있는 수업을 좋아해요. 많은 학생들이 뛰어난 식견을 가지고 있으며 이를 급우들에게 알려 줄 수 있습니다. 저는 이전 토론 수업에서 많은 것을 배웠고 저도 때때로 토론에 기여를 했다고 생각해요. 게다가 토론은 교수가 말만 하는 경우 지루해질 수 있는 수업들을 더 재미있게 만들 수 있습니다.

✎ Summary Notes: Angelina

1) valuable insights
2) insights
3) class discussions
4) own contributions
5) enliven
6) drone on

Organization

Supporting Rudolph's Opinion

1 This is an interesting question that depends upon a person's learning style.

2 Personally, I agree with Rudolph and prefer to listen to lectures.

Answers, Scripts, and Translations **29**

3 My major is history, and I want my professors to spend class telling me about the past.

4 Professors who are well prepared can provide plenty of information in a single class.

5 Plus, I am not particularly interested in class discussions.

6 Students frequently provide incorrect information, such as getting names and dates confused.

7 So they do not help but in fact harm other students, who might get misled by their comments.

8 Overall, it is much better to have lectures than to have discussions.

Supporting Angelina's Opinion

1 Angelina has the right idea as class discussions really can be valuable to students.

2 As she notes, some students make comments that help others.

3 This is particularly true in literature classes, such as when students interpret poems or novels.

4 Thanks to some discussions, I learned to think about poems in new ways.

5 In addition, when a professor guides the discussion, students can learn as much as during a regular lecture.

6 This requires the professor to be an active participant in the discussion and to keep it from getting sidetracked.

7 Still, it can be done.

8 For those two reasons, I prefer classes with discussions to classes that only involve lectures.

Exercise 2 .... p.111

Professor Saville
해석

때때로 개인이나 조직이 대학에 많은 금액을 기부합니다. 이러한 기부금 중 일부는 수백만 달러 혹은 수천만 달러에 이를 수도 있죠. 그러면 대학이 이 돈을 어떻게 쓸 것인지 결정해야 합니다. 새로운 시설을 짓거나 시설을 보수할 수도 있고, 교수진을 확충할 수도 있고, 혹은 그 밖의 다른 일을 할 수도 있을 거예요. 여러분의 생각에는 대학이 많은 기부금을 어떻게 써야 할까요? 그 이유는요?

Francine
해석

학생들에게 장학금 지급을 확대하는 식으로 대학이 그러한 돈을 써야 합니다. 요즘 등록금이 너무 비싸서 많은 학생들이 이를 감당할 수가 없어요. 재정 보조 장학금이라면 크게 환영을 받을 거예요. 학점이 매우 높은 학생들에게 주어지는 성적 우수 장학금도 그렇고요. 이들 학생들은 우수한 성적을 받은 것에 대한 보상을 받아야 하죠.

Anthony
해석

대학은 학생들을 가르치기 위해 존재하는 것이며 이러한 목적은 교수들을 더 많이 채용함으로써 가장 잘 달성될 수 있습니다. 교수의 수가 증가하면 그러한 교수들의 학문적 관심사가 다양할 것이기 때문에 학생들은 더 많은 것을 배우게 될

거예요. 수업 규모도 줄어들 텐데, 그러면 학생들이 교수와 대면할 수 있는 시간이 늘어날 것입니다.

✎ Summary Notes

Francine
1) Students can't afford it
2) Academic scholarships

Anthony
1) Hire more faculty members
2) Class sizes shrink

Sample Response 1 **Supporting New Ideas: Building New Facilities and Making Renovations**

Francine and Anthony each proposes a wonderful idea, but I would choose one suggested by Professor Saville. Our school is in desperate need of new facilities while the old ones should be renovated as well. First of all, there are too many students here and too few buildings. We require more dormitories so that students can live on campus. We also need more buildings in which classes can be taught and research be done. As for existing buildings, many were constructed decades ago. They need to be upgraded and be made more comfortable for students and faculty. Spending the money that way would benefit the most people at school.

해석

Francine과 Anthony 각각 훌륭한 아이디어를 제시했지만 나는 Saville 교수가 제안한 것을 선택하고 싶다. 우리 학교는 새로운 시설이 절실하게 필요한 상태이며 기존 시설들 또한 보수가 되어야 한다. 우선 이곳에는 학생들이 너무 많고 건물들은 너무 적다. 학생들이 캠퍼스에서 지낼 수 있는 기숙사가 더 많이 필요하다. 또한 수업이 진행되고 연구가 수행될 건물들도 더 많이 필요하다. 기존 건물에 대해 말하자면, 많은 건물들이 수십 년 전에 지어졌다. 이러한 건물들은 개선되어야 하며 학생 및 교직원들에게 더 편안한 곳이 되어야 한다. 이러한 식으로 돈을 사용하면 교내 대부분의 사람들에게 혜택이 돌아갈 것이다.

Sample Response 2 **Supporting New Ideas: Upgrading the Library**

Instead of following Francine's or Anthony's suggestions, I would focus on the library. The donated money should be used to increase the library's collection. For one thing, the library lacks many important books and journals. Many students must rely on the interlibrary loan service to get books they need from other schools. Buying more books would give students instant access to them. In addition, the library could upgrade its digital collection. Most e-books are cheaper than physical books. This would let the school purchase numerous books. Our library could instantly go from being below average to being outstanding. That is how I believe the school should spend the money.

해석

Francine이나 Anthony의 제안을 따르는 대신 나는 도서관에 초점을 맞추고자 한다. 기부금은 도서관의 소장 도서를 확충하는데 사용되어야 한다. 우선 도서관에 중요한 도서 및 간행물들이 많지가 않다. 많은 학생들이 도서관 상호 대출 제도에 의존해서 필요한 책을 다른 학교에서 빌리고 있다. 더 많은 도서를 구입한다면 학생들이 곧바로 도서를 이용할 수 있을 것이다. 또한 도서관은 디지털 자료들을 업그레이드할 수 있다. 대부분의 전자책은 실물 도서보다 값이 저렴하다. 이로써 학교측은 다수의 도서를 구입할 수 있을 것이다. 우리 도서관이 즉시 평균 이하의 수준에서 월등한 수준으로 올라갈 수 있을 것이다. 내 생각에 학교측은 바로 이러한 방식으로 돈을 써야 한다.

Unit 14 History of Technology

Exercise 1 ···································· p.114

| Brainstorming & Outlining |

A

Professor Garner

해석

다음 주 수업에서는 변화하고 있는 노동의 속성을 다룰 예정이에요. 예를 들어 전통적으로 사무 노동자들은 매일 사무실에서 근무를 했습니다. 하지만 주로 인터넷 덕분에 사람들은 현재 집에서 근무를 할 수가 있어요. 여러분께 질문을 하나 드리겠습니다. 여러분은 사무실 근무와 재택 근무 중에서 어느 것을 선호하나요? 그 이유는요?

B

Douglas

해석

집에서 일하고 싶은 바람은 이해가 가지만 저는 사무실에서 일하는 것을 선호해요. 동료 직원들과 협력해서 프로젝트를 수행하는 것을 좋아하죠. 이는 제가 사무실에서 일하는 경우에만 가능한 일입니다. 또한 얼굴을 맞대고 일하는 것이 상사로부터 주목을 받을 수 있는 최선의 방법이며, 이로써 승진을 할 수도 있습니다.

⌖ Summary Notes: Douglas

1) collaborating on projects
2) work in office
3) face to face
4) superiors
5) promotions

Kate

해석

저는 재택 근무를 할 수 있는 상황을 선호합니다. 제 부모님들은 모두 장거리 출근을 하시는데, 장시간 운전 후 매일 지친 상태로 퇴근을 하세요. 재택 근무를 하면 통근을 할 필요가 없기 때문에 에너지가 절약될 것입니다. 또한 일을 하거나 개인적인 취미 활동을 할 수 있는 시간도 더 많아질 것이고요.

⌖ Summary Notes: Kate

1) long commutes
2) exhausted
3) driving
4) Avoid
5) energy
6) More time
7) work
8) personal hobbies

| Organization |

Supporting Douglas's Opinion

1 I am in full agreement with Douglas that working in an office is superior to working from home.
2 He is right that face-to-face contact is ideal for getting noticed by managers.
3 I am ambitious and hope to become a CEO one day.
4 To do that, I must become deeply involved in my company's workplace culture.
5 That means I must be in the workplace.
6 Another advantage is that being at work allows people to network.
7 Networking lets people meet others in the same profession, which can lead to personal and professional improvement.
8 In my opinion, the social aspects of being in an office are crucial to succeeding at work.

Supporting Kate's Opinion

1 I understand how Douglas thinks, but I side with Kate.
2 Like Kate's parents, my father once had a long commute.
3 However, he switched to working at home two years ago, and I have never seen him happier.
4 That has resulted in a tremendous improvement in the lives of my entire family.
5 I want that for myself in the future.
6 Additionally, working from home will let me be more productive, so I will work faster than other employees.
7 Being productive, I will likely be promoted rapidly.
8 That will improve my salary and give me financial security.
9 There are simply too many advantages to working at home to turn down that opportunity.

Exercise 2 ···································· p.117

Professor Porter

해석

금요일 수업에서는 인공 지능(AI)에 대해 논의할 것입니다. 미리 그에 대한 여러분들의 생각을 알고 싶군요. AI는 해마다 사회에서 더욱 확산되고 있습니다. AI가 더 발전하면 여러분 생각으로 그것이 인류에게 이로운 영향을 미칠 것 같나요, 아니면 해로운 영향을 미칠 것 같나요? 왜 그렇게 생각하나요?

Yvette
[해석]
저는 AI가 인류에게 긍정적인 영향을 많이 끼칠 것이라고 예상합니다. 예를 들어 이미 AI 프로그램이 사람을 도와 문학 작품과 미술 작품을 만들어 내고 있어요. 이러한 프로그램으로 사람들은 자신의 예술적 능력을 드러낼 수 있습니다. 또한 AI는 수백만 명의 인간에게 도움이 될 새로운 발견을 이끌어 냄으로써 과학자들에게도 도움을 주고 있습니다.

Noah
[해석]
여러 가지 방법으로 AI는 해롭거나 처참한 결과를 가져올 수 있어요. 오늘날 AI는 초기 단계에 있지만, 그럼에도 불구하고 문제들이 있습니다. 학술 보고서 업무를 담당하는 일부 AI는 가짜 연구를 만들어 냅니다. 게다가 AI가 발달할 수록 자기 인식의 가능성도 높아집니다. 그처럼 강력한 AI는 인간을 노예로 삼거나 제거하려 할 수도 있을 거예요.

✏ Summary Notes

Yvette

1) Create written works and art
2) Assist scientists

Noah

1) AIs doing academic reports create fake studies
2) Likely to become self-aware

Sample Response 1 Supporting Yvette

While Noah is smart to be wary of AI, it still has the potential to benefit humans. Yvette points out that AI can make amazing art. I have used AI programs to create my own art, and the results are impressive. They are much better than I could do with paint and a paintbrush. I have also heard that AIs are being used at hospitals to diagnose patients. AIs can take in tons of information and analyze it much faster than a human doctor. This will let patients get swift and accurate diagnoses. As AIs continue to improve, I look forward to seeing more benefits such as these.

[해석]
Noah가 AI를 걱정하는 것은 현명한 일이지만 AI는 인간에게 도움이 될 잠재력을 가지고 있다. Yvette는 AI가 놀라운 예술 작품을 만들 수 있다는 점을 지적한다. 나도 AI 프로그램을 이용해서 그림을 그려본 적이 있는데, 그 결과가 인상적이다. 내가 물감과 붓으로 그릴 수 있는 것보다 훨씬 더 뛰어나다. 나는 또한 AI가 병원에서 환자를 진단하는데 사용되고 있다는 이야기를 들었다. AI는 수많은 정보를 취합해서 인간인 의사보다 훨씬 빨리 정보를 분석할 수 있다. 이로써 환자들은 신속하고 정확한 진단을 받게 될 것이다. AI가 계속 발전하고 있기 때문에 나는 이와 같은 혜택들이 더 많아지기를 고대한다.

Sample Response 2 Supporting Noah

People such as Noah are correct in being concerned about the negative effects of AI. There is a high probability that a super-powered AI that is self-aware would conclude that humans are its enemy. It would therefore decide that to stay alive, it must harm humans. This could result in millions or even billions of deaths on the Earth. Something else to consider is that an AI which is very powerful would almost surely be smarter than humans. It would therefore not be interested in serving humans but would want humans to serve it. I believe there should be strict laws about AI to restrict its development.

[해석]
Noah와 같은 사람들이 AI의 부정적인 영향에 대해 걱정하는 것은 합당한 일이다. 자아 인식을 하는 초강력 AI가 인간은 적이라는 결론을 내릴 가능성이 충분히 있다. 그러면 자신이 살아남기 위해 인간을 공격해야 한다는 결정을 내릴 것이다. 그 결과 지구에서 수백만 혹은 수십억에 이르는 인명 피해가 발생할 수도 있다. 고려해야 할 또 다른 점은 매우 강력한 AI가 거의 확실하게 인간보다 똑똑할 것이라는 점이다. 그러면 인간에게 봉사하려고 하지 않고 인간이 자신에게 봉사하기를 바랄 것이다. 나는 AI의 개발을 제한하는 엄격한 AI 관련법이 존재해야 한다고 생각한다.

Unit 15 Sociology II

Exercise 1 .... p.120

❙ Brainstorming & Outlining ❙

A

Professor Courtland
[해석]
최근에 많은 과학적 발견들이, 특히 의학, 화학, 그리고 물리학에서, 이루어졌습니다. 발견을 한 사람들은 자신이 발견의 결과를 판매함으로써 막대한 돈을 벌고 있어요. 한 가지 질문을 할 테니 생각해 보세요. 중요한 발견이 인류의 이익을 위해 공유되어야 할까요? 아니면 사람과 정부가 그에 따른 수익을 얻는 것이 허용되어야 할까요? 왜 그렇게 생각하나요?

B

Sophie
[해석]
수백만 명의 사람들에게 이익이 될 수 있는 발견을 하면 그러한 발견은 전 세계와 공유하는 것이 의무입니다. 예를 들어 놀라운 효과의 약이 발견되었지만 일부 사람들은 그 가격이 너무 높아서 그 약을 구할 수가 없습니다. 그 결과 그러한 사람들은 살 수 있는데 죽게 됩니다. 이와 같은 불행한 일이 결코 일어나서는 안 됩니다.

Summary Notes: Sophie

1) discoveries
2) millions
3) Duty
4) amazing pharmaceuticals
5) cannot acquire
6) too high
7) die

Stuart

해석

사람들은 과학적인 발견을 이루기 위해 막대한 비용과 때때로 인생의 오랜 시간을 소비합니다. 이들은 투자금을 회수하기 위해 자신의 발견을 현금화할 수 있는 모든 권리를 갖고 있어요. 제한된 기간 동안만 발견에 대한 특허를 유지할 수 있다는 점을 기억합시다. 그 후에는 누구나 사용할 수 있는 권리를 갖게 되죠.

Summary Notes: Stuart

1) make discoveries
2) monetize discoveries
3) Recover
4) time and money
5) patent discoveries
6) limited number
7) use them

| Organization |

Supporting Sophie's Opinion

1 While I understand how Stuart feels, Sophie is correct in stating that important discoveries absolutely must be shared with the world.
2 The first reason is that some of these discoveries could provide immediate benefits to humans.
3 For instance, medicines that can cure fatal diseases must be shared with sick people.
4 The second reason is that scientists can use the discoveries of some people to make discoveries of their own.
5 These new discoveries could provide further advancement for humanity.
6 Think about how many more lives could benefit.
7 These two reasons are why I think discoveries need to be shared with everyone.

Supporting Stuart's Opinion

1 I disagree with Sophie and instead prefer Stuart's argument.
2 When people invest time and money into making a discovery nobody else has, they deserve to profit from it.
3 There is nothing wrong with making money from a discovery.

4 Something else to think about is that if there is no profit motive, then few people will attempt to make new discoveries.
5 After all, why should they work hard if they cannot benefit from the results?
6 When people stop trying to make discoveries, human knowledge will not improve.
7 This will harm society overall.
8 We should therefore permit people to keep the knowledge of their discoveries and to profit from it.

Exercise 2 ·· p.123

Professor Rolfson

해석

여러분도 소셜 미디어에 대해 생각해 보았으면 좋겠어요. 수십억 명의 사람들이 어디에서나 이를 사용하고 있죠. 여기에는 명확한 장점도 존재하지만 단점도 존재해요. 실제로 일부 사람들은 단점 때문에 소셜 미디어가 아이들에게 해로울 수 있다고 주장합니다. 다음 주장을 생각해 보세요. 아이들의 소셜 미디어 사용은 허용되지 않아야 한다. 동의하나요, 동의하지 않나요? 그 이유는요?

Roger

해석

저는 아이들의 소셜 미디어 사용을 허용하지 말아야 한다는 주장에 전적으로 동의합니다. 제게는 남동생 한 명과 여동생 한 명이 있어요. 둘다 소셜 미디어에 중독되어 있죠. 항상 소셜 미디어 페이지에 사진을 업로드하고 자신의 근황을 적고 있지만 학업과 집안일은 소홀히 해요. 제 동생들은, 다른 아이들도 마찬가지로, 분명 책임감이 너무 없기 때문에 소셜 미디어를 사용해서는 안 됩니다.

Wilma

해석

아이들에게 소셜 미디어를 금지시킬 필요는 없어요. 실제로 아이들은 그로 인해 많은 혜택을 얻을 수 있습니다. 예를 들어 컴퓨터 사용법을 배울 수도 있고 친구 및 친척들과 커뮤니케이션을 할 수도 있어요. 일부가 과도하게 사용할 수도 있겠지만 그러한 경우에는 부모가 개입을 하면 되죠. 모든 아이들에게 소셜 미디어를 금지시키는 것은 과도한 대응일 거예요.

Summary Notes

Roger

1) Addicted to social media
2) Neglect homework and chores

Wilma

1) Communicate w/friends + relatives
2) Prohibiting all children = overreaction

Sample Response 1 Supporting Roger

Although Wilma makes some good points, Roger has the right idea in wanting to ban children from using social media. As he points out, social media is highly addictive. I used it for hours and hours each day in my youth. It caused considerable harm until my parents forced me to delete my accounts. Unfortunately, many parents are not as involved in the lives of their children as mine were.

Plus, many parents work and get home late at night. So they cannot stop their children from logging on to social media sites. This means that the best action is to ban children from using it.

해석

Wilma가 좋은 지적을 하고 있지만 아이들의 소셜 미디어 사용을 금지해야 한다는 Roger의 생각이 옳다. 그가 지적한 대로 소셜 미디어는 매우 중독적이다. 나도 어렸을 때 하루에 몇 시간씩 소셜 미디어를 사용했다. 부모님께서 강제로 내 계정을 삭제하시기 전까지 엄청난 피해를 가져다 주었다. 안타깝게도 많은 부모들이 내 경우와 달리 아이들의 생활에 관여를 하지 않는다. 게다가 많은 부모들은 일을 해서 밤 늦게 집으로 돌아온다. 그래서 아이들이 소셜 미디어 사이트에 접속하는 것을 막을 수가 없다. 이는 최선의 조치가 아이들의 소셜 미디어 사용을 금지하는 것이라는 점을 의미한다.

Sample Response 2 Supporting Wilma

I see no reason to ban children from social media, so I disagree with the statement. Children can benefit from social media. As Wilma writes, it is a great way for children to keep in touch with their friends and relatives. They can get regular updates on those people's lives. Additionally, a recent study has shown that the brains of children who use social media develop better than those of children who watch TV and play computer games. There is clearly a benefit to using social media that will help children for their entire lives. I therefore disagree that children should be banned from social media.

해석

아이들의 소셜 미디어 사용을 금지할 어떤 이유도 찾을 수 없기 때문에 나는 그러한 주장에 동의하지 않는다. 아이들은 소셜 미디어로 혜택을 받을 수 있다. Wilma가 쓴 것과 같이 소셜 미디어는 아이들이 친구 및 친척들과 연락을 주고받을 수 있는 좋은 방법이다. 정기적으로 그들의 삶에 대한 소식을 받을 수 있다. 또한 최근 연구에 따르면 소셜 미디어를 사용하는 아이들의 뇌가 TV를 보고 컴퓨터 게임을 하는 아이들의 뇌보다 더 잘 발달한다. 따라서 소셜 미디어 사용에는 분명한 혜택이 존재하며, 이는 아이들에게 평생에 걸쳐 도움이 될 것이다. 그러므로 나는 아이들의 소셜 미디어 사용을 금지해야 한다는 주장에 동의하지 않는다.

Unit 16 Health

Exercise 1 .... p.126

‖ Brainstorming & Outlining ‖

A

Professor McCloud

해석

다음 수업 시간에는 의약품 접근권에 대해 논의할 예정입니다. 여러분들이 다음과 같은 점을 생각해 보면 좋을 것 같군요. 많은 약들이 발견되어 있습니다. 하지

만 일부는 사람들이 구하기가 힘들어요. 특정 의약품들을 처방전을 통해서만 구할 수 있어야 한다고 생각하나요? 아니면 원하는 어떤 약이던 사람들이 구입할 수 있어야 할까요? 그 이유는요?

B

Florence

해석

현재 몇몇 의약품은 극도로 강해서 면허가 있는 의사로부터 처방전을 받은 후에만 구입이 가능합니다. 이러한 약을 복용하는 사람들은 약에 중독될 수 있고 또한 심각한 부작용을 겪을 수도 있어요. 이러한 의약품들은 사람들이 피해를 입지 않도록 규제하는 것이 중요합니다.

✒️ **Summary Notes: Florence**

1) extremely potent
2) prescribed
3) licensed doctor
4) addicted
5) side effects
6) regulate
7) suffering harm

Arnold

해석

자신이 원하는 약을 복용하는 사람들에게는 아무런 문제가 없습니다. 약국은 처방전이 없어도 보유하고 있는 모든 약을 판매할 수 있어야 해요. 하지만 약사들은 개인들에게 두 가지를, 즉 약을 적절하게 복용하는 법과 그 약이 어떤 부작용을 일으킬 수 있는지를 알려 주어야 할 것입니다.

✒️ **Summary Notes: Arnold**

1) take any medicine
2) drugstores
3) prescription
4) pharmacists
5) take medicine properly
6) side effects

‖ Organization ‖

Supporting Florence's Opinion

1 This is a controversial issue, but I know where I stand on it.
2 I am like Florence and believe certain medicines should require a prescription before people can acquire them.
3 As Florence notes, some medications are highly addictive.
4 This is especially true of painkillers.
5 People who receive easy access to these medicines frequently ruin their lives.
6 Something else to think about is that mixing medicines can be harmful.
7 By that, I mean that when people take multiple

medicines simultaneously, they can suffer serious health problems.

8   Doctors know about this issue, so they are always careful when prescribing medicine.

9   That is why prescriptions are necessary.

Supporting Arnold's Opinion

1   Arnold is correct that people should be allowed to purchase any medications they want.

2   If a pharmacy carries a medicine, any customer should be permitted to purchase it.

3   Many countries do not require prescriptions, so people can buy any medications.

4   The people in these countries are not suffering major problems.

5   People in my country should get to acquire any medicine they want as well.

6   In addition, thanks to the Internet, many people self-diagnose their problems.

7   They should not have to visit a doctor to get a prescription when they know what their problem is.

8   That is a waste of time and money.

9   Clearly, prescriptions are not necessary anymore.

Exercise 2 .... p.129

Professor Gustav
해석

모두가 건강 보험에 대해 생각해 보면 좋을 것 같군요. 최근에 건강 보험료가 극적으로 인상되었습니다. 일부 사람들은 입원 및 수술 후에 수천 달러에 이르는 청구서를 받고 있죠. 이는 많은 가정에 경제적인 부담이 되고 있습니다. 다음과 같은 점을 생각해 보세요. 건강 보험은 전부 무료여야 한다. 여기에 동의하나요, 동의하지 않나요? 그 이유는요?

Ivan
해석

저는 건강 보험이 무료여야 한다는 점에 동의합니다. 최근에 제 삼촌께서 일주일 동안 병원에 입원하셨어요. 의료 보험이 없었기 때문에 진료비로 90,000달러 이상이 청구되었죠. 삼촌께서는 그처럼 엄청난 금액을 감당하실 수가 없으세요. 우리나라의 수많은 사람들이 비슷한 상황에 직면해 있습니다. 건강 보험이 무료라면 값비싼 진료비에 대해 걱정하지 않아도 될 거예요.

Caroline
해석

막대한 진료비를 청구받은 사람들의 심정은 이해하지만 저는 그러한 주장에 동의하지 않습니다. 무료 건강 보험은 사실 무료가 아니에요. 누군가가 그에 대한 비용을 지불해야 하며 바로 그 누군가는 우리나라의 납세자들입니다. 우리나라에서 건강 보험이 무료가 된다면 의사와 병원에 비용을 지급하기 위해 세금이 인상될 거예요. 저는 다른 사람의 의료 서비스에 대한 비용을 내고 싶지 않습니다.

✎ Summary Notes

Ivan

1) Inflated price → can't pay off

2) If have free health care, no expensive bills

Caroline

1) Free health care = not really free

2) Need to pay doctors and hospitals

Sample Response 1 Supporting Ivan

While many people oppose the concept of free health care, I am not one of them. Ivan explains perfectly why I support free health care for everyone. Too many people get stuck with massive amounts of debt after receiving medical treatment. Hospitals have such expensive rates that most people cannot afford them. The price of health insurance has also gone up considerably lately. Many families pay more than one thousand dollars a month on medical insurance. Yet they must still pay money when they require medical treatment. This is not sustainable, so the government needs to act. Providing free health care is the best solution.

해석

많은 사람들이 무료 건강 보험의 개념을 반대하지만 나는 그러한 사람 중 한 명이 아니다. Ivan은 내가 모든 사람에게 의료 보험료가 무료여야 한다는 점을 지지하는 이유를 완벽하게 설명하고 있다. 너무나 많은 사람들이 의학적인 치료를 받은 후 엄청난 빚더미에 앉게 된다. 병원 진료비가 너무 높아서 대부분의 사람들이 이를 감당할 수 없다. 건강 보험료 또한 최근에 상당히 인상되었다. 많은 가정이 의료 보험으로 한 달에 천 달러 이상을 내고 있다. 하지만 그럼에도 불구하고 의학적인 치료가 필요한 경우에는 돈을 내야 한다. 이는 지속 가능한 일이 아니며 따라서 정부가 조치를 취해야 한다. 건강 보험을 무료로 제공하는 것이 최선의 방안이다.

Sample Response 2 Supporting Caroline

If I had to choose one of these options, I would oppose free health care. As Caroline remarks, there is no such thing as free. Taxpayers would be stuck with the bill, which would be enormous. We already lose a huge part of our paychecks to taxes. Getting taxed more would not be helpful. What people should do is acquire medical insurance. It is possible to get plans that cover catastrophic events, such as car accidents. Then, if people have a medical emergency, they will not suddenly go into debt. People ought to take responsibility for their own lives and stop demanding that others pay for their expenses.

해석

두 가지 방안 중 하나를 선택해야 한다면 나는 무료 건강 보험을 반대하고자 한다. Caroline이 언급한 것처럼 공짜인 것은 없다. 납세자들이 억지로 비용을 부담하게 될 텐데, 그 비용은 막대할 것이다. 우리 급여의 상당 부분이 이미 세금으로 떼이고 있다. 세금을 더 걷는 것은 도움이 되지 않을 것이다. 사람들이 해야 하는 일은 의료 보험에 가입하는 것이다. 자동차 사고와 같은 재해를 보장해 주는 보험에 가입할 수 있다. 그러면 위급한 의료 상황에 처한 경우 갑자기 빚을 지게 되지는 않을 것이다. 사람들은 본인의 생명을 책임져야 하며 다른 사람들이 그 비용을 내도록 요구해서는 안 된다.

Actual Test

Task 1

| Reading |

해석

현대로 접어들면서 사람들의 생활 방식에 많은 발전이 이루어졌지만 한 가지 부정적인 측면도 나타났다. 바로 미국의 자녀 양육비가 급등했다는 점이다. 실제로 미국에서 자녀를 양육하려면 지구상의 어느 나라에서보다도 비용이 많이 든다.

최근 조사에 따르면 부모들은, 아이가 태어난 순간부터 약 21세의 나이로 대학을 졸업할 때까지, 먹이고 입히고 교육시키는데 평균적으로 대략 26만 달러를 써야 한다. 많은 가정의 경우, 자녀를 값비싼 사립 학교 및 대학에 보내기 때문에 그 비용은 훨씬 올라가는데, 일부 학교는 등록금과 기숙사비로 연간 80,000달러 이상을 요구하고 있다. 이러한 수치에 여행이나 장난감, 그리고 기타 완구는 포함되어 있지 않으며, 이것들 역시 비용이 상당할 수 있다.

믿기 힘들지만 미국에서 아이를 키우려면 프랑스 및 스페인과 같은 다른 서구 국가에 비해 3분의 1 정도의 돈이 더 필요하다. 그러한 이유 중 하나는 많은 유럽 국가에서 제한된 사회주의가 확립되어 있기 때문으로, 이러한 곳에서는 아이를 학교에 보내는 비용을 부모가 부담하지 않아도 된다. 또한 이러한 국가들의 생활 수준은 미국보다 낮지만 물가 또한 저렴한 편이라서, 이러한 점이 큰 장점으로 작용해 부모들이 보다 많은 돈을 저축할 수 있다.

마지막으로 부모가 돈을 지출하는 분야에 관한 문제가 있다. 대다수 국가들의 부모들은 아이를 위해 쓰는 돈의 대부분을 옷과 음식 같은 필수품에 쓴다. 하지만 미국인들은 다른 나라 사람들이 과도하다고 생각할 수도 있는 품목에 돈을 쓰고 있다. 예를 들어 미국의 부모들은 학업, 음악, 그리고 체육에 대한 개인 교습에 상당한 비용을 지출한다. 또한 자녀의 건강 보험료로 막대한 비용을 지출한다. 이 모든 이유들 때문에 미국에서 아이를 기르면 매우 많은 돈이 든다.

| Listening |

Script 🎧 02-03

W Professor: Everyone knows that raising children in the United States is expensive nowadays. Indeed, that's one reason why many couples are choosing to have only one child or none at all. However, I don't want to discourage any of you from having children of your own. There are some ways to get those expenses down.

For example, many families, even those with health insurance, spend huge amounts of money on medical expenses for their children. That's understandable. But instead of treating illnesses when they occur, they ought to be practicing prevention, which, in the long run, will save them money. One way to do this is to practice extreme cleanliness. A clean child is a healthy child. Clean children become sick less often and have fewer allergies. That's money in the bank right there.

Another cost-reducing measure is also related to health. We often hear about kids that get burned in the kitchen or hurt themselves in other ways. Remember that even with health insurance, one trip to the hospital can cost tens of thousands of dollars. So parents should be educating their children on safety. Knowing about safety increases the chances that a child won't get hurt and will remain out of harm.

Finally, parents should be encouraging their children to pursue their own intellectual interests. Too many times, parents waste money on tutoring or lessons that their children aren't interested in. Why pay for piano lessons if your kid hates the piano? He's not going to become the next Mozart if he hates it. And parents shouldn't spend so much money on educational software if it's for something that their child has no interest in. Of course, these suggestions might only reduce a few thousand dollars off the total price tag, but at today's rates, every dollar counts.

해석

W Professor: 요즘 미국의 자녀 양육비가 높다는 점은 모두가 알고 있어요. 실제로 이는 많은 부부들이 한 명의 자녀만 갖거나 아예 자녀를 갖지 않는 이유 중 하나이기도 하죠. 하지만 저는 여러분에게 자녀를 갖지 말라고 권하고 싶지는 않습니다. 그러한 비용을 줄일 수 있는 몇 가지 방법이 있어요.

예를 들어 많은 가정들이, 심지어 의료 보험에 가입된 가정들도, 자녀에게 막대한 의료비를 지출합니다. 이해할 수 있는 일이에요. 하지만 질병이 발생해서 치료하는 것 대신에 예방을 해야 하는데, 장기적으로는, 그렇게 해야 비용이 절약이 될 것입니다. 그럴 수 있는 한 가지 방법은 청결을 유지하는 것이에요. 청결한 아이는 건강합니다. 청결한 아이는 병에 걸리는 경우가 적고 알레르기 반응이 나타나는 경우도 적죠. 돈이 은행에 그대로 있게 됩니다.

비용을 절감할 수 있는 또 다른 방법 역시 건강과 관련된 것이에요. 우리는 종종 부엌에서 화상을 입거나 기타 방식으로 다치는 아이들에 대한 이야기를 듣습니다. 의료 보험이 있더라도 병원을 한 번 찾게 되면 수만 달러가 들 수도 있다는 점을 기억하세요. 따라서 부모들이 자녀에게 안전 교육을 시켜야 합니다. 안전에 대해 알게 되면 자녀가 부상을 입지 않고 안전하게 있을 수 있는 가능성이 높아지죠.

마지막으로 부모들은 자녀들이 각자 가진 지적 관심 분야를 파고들 수 있도록 장려해야 해요. 매우 많은 경우, 부모들은 자녀들이 흥미를 느끼지 않는 개인 과외나 레슨 수업에 돈을 낭비하고 있습니다. 아이가 피아노를 싫어하는데 왜 피아노 레슨에 돈을 쓰나요? 피아노를 싫어하는 아이가 모차르트처럼 되지는 않을 거예요. 그리고 부모들은 자녀들이 관심을 보이지 않는 교육용 소프트웨어에 그렇게 많은 돈을 써서는 안 됩니다. 물론 이러한 제안들이 전체 비용에서 불과 수천 달러를 절약시켜 주는 정도일 수도 있지만, 현재의 상황에서는 1달러도 중요합니다.

Sample Response

The reading passage states that the cost of raising children in the United States is higher than in other countries. The professor, however, claims there are many ways to decrease these costs.

The reading mentions that raising a child from birth to college averages more than 300,000 dollars. It declares that this number is often higher and does not include expenses like travel or toys. The professor notes that healthcare costs are enormous. She says that if parents practice prevention and keep their children clean and healthy, they can save lots of money.

The reading then argues that American tuition rates are much higher than in Europe, where many attend school for free. It also states that products in these countries are cheaper than in the U.S. However, the professor counters by saying parents should educate their children about safety. This will keep their children from getting hurt and will save thousands in medical expenses.

Finally, responding to the claim that American parents spend more money on excessive or unnecessary items, the professor declares that parents should first learn what their children enjoy before paying for it. For example, parents should not pay for piano lessons if their child hates playing the piano.

The professor comes up with several ways to decrease the price of raising a child, thereby making having children more appealing to couples.

해석

읽기 지문에는 미국의 자녀 양육비가 다른 국가에 비해 높다고 나와 있다. 하지만 교수는 이러한 비용을 줄일 수 있는 여러 가지 방법이 있다고 주장한다.

읽기 지문은 한 명의 자녀가 태어나 대학에 갈 때까지 드는 양육비가 평균적으로 300,000달러 이상이라고 말한다. 이러한 수치는 종종 더 높아지기도 하며, 여행이나 장난감 등의 비용은 여기에 포함되어 있지 않다고 나와 있다. 교수는 의료비가 엄청나게 많이 든다는 점을 지적한다. 그녀는 부모들이 예방 조치를 취해서 자녀들을 청결하고 건강하게 키우면 많은 비용을 절약할 수 있다고 말한다.

이후 읽기 지문은 미국의 등록금이 유럽에 비해 훨씬 높다고 주장하는데, 유럽에서는 많은 학생들이 무료로 학교에 다닌다. 또한 이러한 국가들의 상품 가격이 미국보다 저렴하고 말한다. 하지만 교수는 부모들이 안전에 관해 자녀들을 교육해야 한다고 말함으로써 그러한 주장을 반박한다. 그렇게 하면 자녀가 다치는 것을 막고 수천 달러의 의료비를 절약하게 될 것이다.

마지막으로 미국 부모들이 과도하거나 불필요한 부분에 더 많은 돈을 쓰고 있다는 주장에 대해 교수는 부모들이 돈을 쓰기 전에 자녀들이 배우고 싶어하는 것이 무엇인지를 먼저 살펴야 한다고 주장한다. 예를 들어 자녀가 피아노 치는 것을 싫어하는 경우, 부모들은 피아노 레슨을 시켜서는 안 된다.

교수는 자녀 양육비를 줄임으로써 부부들에게 자녀 양육이 보다 매력적으로 보이게 만들 수 있는 몇 가지 방법을 제시하고 있다.

Task 2

Professor Bannon
해석

여러 도심지에서 정부들이 도로를 제대로 관리하지 못하고 있습니다. 정부 관계자들은 보수할 수 있는 자금이 부족하다고 주장을 해요. 도로 보수를 위한 자금을 마련해야 한다고 주장하죠. 그러면 제가 여러분에게 질문을 하나 하겠습니다. 시내의 모든 주요 도로들을 유료화해야 한다고 생각하나요? 그 이유는요?

Lucinda
해석

저는 시내의 주요 도로들을 유료 도로로 만드는 것이 멋진 아이디어라고 생각해요. 하지만 통행료로 마련되는 모든 돈은 도로 자체에 쓰여야 할 것입니다. 정부 관계자들이 돈의 목적을 변경해서 다른 일에 쓰는 것은 허용되지 않아야 해요. 도로를 유료화함으로써 시내 도로의 상태가 개선될 것이며, 이로 인해 수많은 사람들이 혜택을 받게 될 것입니다.

Walter
해석

저는 사람들이 어렵게 번 돈을 정부가 계속해서 빼앗아 가려고 한다는 점에 신물이 납니다. 우리는 이미 충분히 많은 세금을 내고 있는데 정부는 지금 단지 도로 보수를 위해 우리가 돈을 더 내기를 바란다고요? 저는 받아들일 수 없습니다. 정부가 돈을 낭비하는 일을 멈춘다면 도로를 보수할 수 있는 충분한 자금이 마련될 것입니다.

Sample Response 1 Supporting Lucinda

I understand Walter's argument, but I believe Lucinda's is more correct. As she mentions, city roads could be maintained well if there were enough money. A great way to raise money is to make major roads in urban centers toll roads. The tolls would not have to be very high, especially for roads that many drivers use. I have visited some places with many toll roads. The roads were all in perfect condition and lacked potholes. I wish our city's roads resembled those. I sympathize with Walter's arguments because taxes are too high. Nevertheless, I do not mind paying extra for a good cause, which having well-maintained roads is.

해석

Walter의 주장도 이해가 가지만 나는 Lucinda의 주장이 더 적절하다고 생각한다. 그녀가 언급한 대로 시내 도로는 충분한 돈이 있을 때 잘 관리될 수 있다. 돈을 마련할 수 있는 좋은 방법은 도심지의 주요 도로들을 유료 도로로 만드는 것이다. 통행료는, 특히 많은 운전자들이 사용하는 도로의 경우, 크게 비싸지 않을 것이다. 나는 유료 도로가 많은 몇몇 지역을 방문한 적이 있었다. 모든 도로들의 상태가 완벽했고 포트 홀도 없었다. 나는 이곳 시내 도로들도 그와 비슷하면 좋겠다. 세금이 너무 높다는 점에서 나는 Walter의 주장에도 공감이 간다. 그럼에도 불구하고 나는 정당한 명분, 즉 잘 관리되는 도로를 위해서라면 추가적인 부담도 개의하지 않는다.

Sample Response 2 Supporting Walter

Although Lucinda's argument makes sense, Walter is correct. Our taxes are already high enough, so the government should not tax us more to use city roads. Walter also points out that government officials waste too much money. They receive plenty of funds, so there should be no need to make people pay tolls for local roads. Let me add that one of the purposes of the government is to provide basic transportation for people. This means the government must take care of roads. It can cancel some unnecessary government spending programs and then use the money saved to fix the roads. Then, drivers will not have to pay any tolls.

해석

Lucinda의 주장에도 일리가 있지만 Walter가 옳다. 세금이 이미 충분히 높기 때문에 정부는 도로 사용에 대한 세금을 더 부과해서는 안 된다. Walter는 또한 정부 관계자들이 너무 많은 돈을 낭비한다는 점을 지적한다. 그들은 많은 자금을 받고 있기 때문에 사람들에게 인근 도로의 통행료를 내라고 할 필요가 전혀 없다. 덧붙여 말하면 정부의 목표 중 하나는 사람들에게 기본적인 교통 수단을 제공하는 것이다. 이는 정부가 도로에 신경을 써야 한다는 점을 의미한다. 불필요한 정부 지출 프로그램을 취소하고 그 돈을 모아 도로 보수에 쓸 수 있다. 그러면 운전자들이 통행료를 납부할 필요가 없을 것이다.

Actual Test 02

Task 1

| Reading |

해석

요즘 법 집행과 관련된 가장 논란의 여지가 많은 것 중 하나는 과속 단속 카메라이다. 이 카메라는 다양한 장소에 설치되어 지나가는 차량의 속도를 측정하는 데 사용된다. 카메라에는 레이더 감지기가 설치되어 있어서 카메라가 과속 차량의 사진을 찍은 후 위반 차량 운전자에게 과속 딱지를 보내어 추후에 벌금을 납부하도록 만든다. 많은 사람들이 과속 단속 카메라를 싫어하지만 이 카메라는 실제로 사회에 유익하다.

우선, 과속 단속 카메라 덕분에 도로가 더욱 안전해졌다. 때로는 단속 카메라가 근처에 있다는 표시가 있기도 하지만 대부분의 경우 카메라는 보이지 않는 곳에 숨겨져 있다. 따라서 운전자가 근처에 단속 카메라가 있다고 느끼거나 카메라가 있다고 아는 경우에는 운전자들이 대개 속도를 늦추는데, 그 이유는 과속 위반 딱지의 벌금이 200달러 이상이기 때문이다. 속도가 낮다는 것은 사고가 적다는 의미이므로 과속 단속 카메라는 이미 사람들을 보호하는데 도움을 주고 있다.

둘째, 과속 단속 카메라 덕분에 경찰들이 과속 운전자를 찾느라 많은 시간을 낭비할 필요가 없다. 이로써 자유로워진 경찰들은 범인을 잡고 대중의 안전을 도모하는 것과 같은 다른 중요한 일들을 할 수가 있다. 실제로 과속 단속 카메라의 성공으로 더 많은 카메라가 설치되고 있기 때문에 미래에는 경찰관이 과속 위반 딱지를 떼는 경우가 완전히 없어질지도 모른다.

마지막으로, 과속 단속 카메라는 실제로 과속을 했다는 확실한 증거를 제공해주기 때문에 법정에서 과속 위반 딱지에 항의하는 사람들이 줄어들었다. 이러한 불만 감소로 인해 항상 사건들로 일이 밀려 있던 교통 위반 즉결 재판소가 한가하기 시작했다. 대다수 위반자들이 위반 장면이 찍힌 사진을 우편으로 받으면 항의를 하는 대신 수표를 끊어서 벌금을 낸다.

| Listening |

Script 🎧 02-06

M Professor: I must say that I find speed cameras to be some of the most abhorrent devices that police departments all across the country are using. Not only do they infringe upon our basic rights, but they are also inherently dangerous. Here, let me give you a few reasons as to why I feel this way.

First of all, speed cameras actually don't make the roads safer. They make the roads more dangerous in many cases. Why? Let me explain. People are often worried about getting a speeding ticket since they cost so much money. So if a person is speeding and suddenly notices a camera, what's he going to do? Slam on the brakes. That's what. And then the car behind him might just slam into him. There are numerous documented cases of accidents occurring because people tried suddenly to slow down upon seeing a traffic camera. Traffic cameras clearly aren't saving lives. In some cases, they are ending lives.

Here's another thing. Now that fewer police officers are being tasked to catching speeders, they have more time to snoop around and bother law-abiding citizens. Just the other week, I was harassed in the park by a cop when all I was doing was sitting on a bench and feeding the squirrels. And you'll notice that crime rates haven't decreased since speed cameras have been installed. So what are the cops doing with their extra time?

Finally, cameras malfunction. Several people have received pictures in the mail that weren't even their cars. And others have gotten ticketed when they were definitely not speeding. Simply put, these cameras cannot be trusted to be completely accurate, and the government would be wise to ban their use before they cause any more problems.

해석

M Professor: 사실 저는 과속 단속 카메라가 미국 전역의 경찰들이 사용하는 장비 중에서 가장 혐오스러운 것이라고 생각해요. 우리의 기본적인 권리를 침해할 뿐만 아니라 본질적으로 위험하기까지 하죠. 제가 그렇게 생각하는 몇 가지 이유를 말씀드리겠습니다.

우선 과속 단속 카메라 때문에 실제로 도로가 더 안전한 것은 아니에요. 많은 경우 도로를 더 위험하게 만듭니다. 왜 그럴까요? 설명해 드리죠. 사람들은 돈을 많이 내야 하기 때문에 종종 과속 위반 딱지를 받을까 걱정을 합니다. 어떤 사람이 과속을 하다가 과속 단속 카메라를 발견하면 그가 어떻게 할까요? 급히 브레이크를 밟습니다. 그렇습니다. 그 후에는 뒤따르던 차가 그 차와 충돌할 수도 있어요. 과속 단속 카메라를 본 사람이 갑자기 속도를 늦춰서 발생했던 사고들의 기록이 많습니다. 그러니 과속 단속 카메라가 생명을 구하고 있지는 않아요. 일부 경우 생명을 앗아가고 있습니다.

또 다른 이유도 있어요. 과속 위반자를 잡는 일에 투입되는 경찰관이 줄어들면 이들이 여기저기를 기웃거리고 다니면서 법을 준수하는 시민들을 못살게 굴수 있는 시간이 늘어납니다. 지난 주에 저는 다람쥐에게 먹이를 주면서 벤치에 앉아 있었는데, 한 경찰관이 공원에서 저를 괴롭히더군요. 과속 단속 카메라가 설치된 이후 범죄 발생률이 줄지 않았다는 점도 여러분이 알게 될 것입니다. 그러면 남는 시간 동안 경찰은 무엇을 하고 있을까요?

마지막으로, 과속 단속 카메라는 오작동을 합니다. 어떤 사람들은 자신의 차 사진이 아닌 사진을 우편으로 받기도 했어요. 그리고 분명히 과속을 하지 않았는데 과속 위반 딱지를 떼인 사람도 있습니다. 간단히 말해서 이들 과속 단속 카메라가 전적으로 정확하다고 믿어서는 안 되며, 정부는 과속 단속 카메라가 더 이상의 문제를 일으키기 전에 그 사용을 금지시키는 편이 좋을 것입니다.

Sample Response

The reading passage makes the argument that speed cameras are beneficial to society. The professor, however, argues that they strip people of their rights and are actually dangerous.

First, the reading claims that speed cameras make roads safer because people will drive slowly for fear of paying heavy fines. Because they are driving slower, they have few accidents. The professor, however, says that speed cameras make roads more dangerous. According to him, people who are speeding will slow down suddenly upon seeing a camera, thereby often causing accidents as they try to avoid getting ticketed.

The reading also states that speed cameras allow officers to spend more time catching criminals instead of watching for speeders. The professor counters this argument by mentioning that police are starting to harass law-abiding citizens like him. He also adds that crime rates have not decreased lately, so the police are obviously not doing much with this extra time.

Finally, while the reading claims that the backlog of court cases is decreasing as fewer people protest their tickets in courts because of speed cameras, the professor says that many people are being improperly fined, so speed cameras cannot be trusted. For this reason, he believes they should be banned.

해석

읽기 지문은 과속 단속 카메라가 사회에 유익하다고 주장한다. 하지만 교수는 과속 단속 카메라가 사람들의 권리를 빼앗으며 실제로 위험한 것이라고 주장한다.

먼저 읽기 지문은 사람들이 비싼 벌금을 내는 것을 두려워하기 때문에 과속 단속 카메라가 도로를 더 안전하게 만든다고 주장한다. 운전을 천천히 하기 때문에 사고가 줄어든다. 하지만 교수는 과속 단속 카메라로 인해 도로가 더 위험해진다고 말한다. 그에 따르면 과속을 하던 사람은 과속 단속 카메라를 보고 갑자기 속도를 늦추려고 할 텐데, 그 결과 위반 딱지를 피하려다가 종종 교통 사고를 유발하게 된다.

읽기 지문은 또한 과속 단속 카메라 덕분에 경찰들이 속도 위반자를 지켜보는 대신 다른 범인을 잡는데 더 많은 시간을 투입할 수 있다고 말한다. 교수는 경찰들이 자신처럼 법을 준수하는 시민들을 괴롭히기 시작했다고 말함으로써 그러한 주장을 반박한다. 그는 또한 최근에 범죄 발생률이 감소하지 않았기 때문에 경찰들이 그처럼 남는 시간에 분명 많은 일을 하고 있지는 않을 것이라고 덧붙여 말한다.

마지막으로 읽기 지문은 과속 단속 카메라 덕분에 교통 위반 즉결 재판소에서 위반 딱지에 대해 항의하는 사람들이 감소함으로써 재판소에 적체된 소송 업무가 줄고 있다고 주장하지만, 교수는 많은 사람들이 부당하게 벌금을 부과받기 때문에 단속 카메라를 신뢰할 수 없다고 말한다. 이러한 이유에서 그는 과속 단속 카메라 사용이 중단되어야 한다고 생각한다.

Task 2

Professor Whittaker
해석

잠깐 스포츠에 대해 생각해 보죠. 사람들은 팀 스포츠와 개인 스포츠 모두 할 수 있어요. 일반적으로 실내 및 야외 스포츠를 하는 사람들은 다양한 기술과 능력을 익힙니다. 두 가지 유형의 스포츠 중에서 십대가 하기에 어느 것이 더 좋을까요? 그러한 스포츠를 함으로써 어떤 기술을 익힐 수 있을까요?

Leonardo
해석

저는 십대였을 때 팀 스포츠인 축구와 농구를 했습니다. 이들은 분명 골프와 볼링과 같은 개인 스포츠보다 뛰어나며 십대들에 큰 도움이 되죠. 이러한 스포츠에 참여하면 틀림없이 팀워크를 배우게 됩니다. 함께 경기를 잘 하지 않으면 팀이 질 수가 있죠. 팀 스포츠는 또한 전략을 요구하는데, 따라서 십대들이 경기에서 승리하기 위한 계획을 세우는 법을 익히게 됩니다.

Shannon
해석

두 유형의 스포츠 모두 십대들에게 유익해서 저는 모든 십대들이 스포츠에 참여해야 하기를 바랍니다. 하지만 십대들에게는 개인 스포츠가 더 낫습니다. 먼저 선수가 승리하기 위해서는 자신 이외의 다른 사람에게 의지할 수가 없습니다. 따라서 자립심을 익히게 됩니다. 또한 자신감이 증가할 수도 있어요. 어쨌거나 승리를 하는 경우에 그러한 승리의 공로가 전적으로 자신에게 있다는 점을 알게 되죠.

Sample Response 1 Supporting Leonardo

Leonardo and Shannon make good arguments on behalf of team and individual sports. I, like Leonardo, participated in team sports and learned various skills playing them. For that reason, I truly believe team sports are better for teens. How to cooperate with others is the best skill they can learn. Even if they dislike a teammate, players learn to work together with that person to win a game. Players also learn communication skills. Players must talk to one another in basketball, soccer, and football games. They communicate about strategy and what they need to do. Those skills are more important than those they learn from individual sports.

해석

Leonardo와 Shannon은 팀 스포츠와 개인 스포츠를 대변하면서 좋은 주장을 펴고 있다. 나는 Leonardo와 마찬가지로 팀 스포츠에 참여했고 경기를 하면서 다양한 기술을 익혔다. 그러한 이유에서 나는 진정으로 십대들에게 팀 스포츠가 더 적합하다고 생각한다. 다른 사람과 협동하는 기술이 그들이 배울 수 있는 최고의 기술이다. 선수들은 팀 동료가 마음에 들지 않더라도 경기에서 승리하기 위해서는 그 사람과 협력해야 한다는 점을 알게 된다. 또한 선수들은 커뮤니케이션 기술을 익히게 된다. 농구, 축구, 그리고 미식축구 경기에서 선수들은 서로 이야기를 나누어야 한다. 전략과 자신들의 역할에 대해 커뮤니케이션을 한다. 이러한 기술은 개인 스포츠에서 익힐 수 있는 기술보다 중요한 것이다.

Sample Response 2 Supporting Shannon

I believe teens can learn more from individual sports such as tennis and swimming. Shannon mentions self-reliance and confidence, two important attributes. Let me add that participants in individual sports also learn to focus better. If they cannot focus, they have no way to win. When a person wins a golf or tennis match, that person's self-esteem improves, too. After all, he or she was solely responsible for the victory. Knowing that will make the winner feel great. Leonardo is correct in that team sports teach valuable skills like teamwork. But we live in an individualist society. So doing well at individual sports can prepare teens for the future.

해석

나는 십대들이 테니스와 수영과 같은 개인 스포츠에서 더 많이 배울 수 있다고 생각한다. Shannon은 두 가지 중요한 자질인 자립심과 자신감을 언급한다. 덧붙여 말하면 개인 스포츠의 참가자들은 또한 집중하는 법을 배우게 된다. 집중을 하지 못하면 결코 승리하지 못한다. 골프나 테니스 경기에서 승리하는 경우에는 그 사람의 자부심 역시 커지게 된다. 어쨌거나 승리에 대한 공로는 오로지 자신에게 있었다. 그런 점을 알면 우승자는 엄청난 자부심을 느끼게 될 것이다. 팀 스포츠가 팀워크와 같은 귀중한 기술을 가르쳐 준다는 Leonardo의 말은 맞다. 하지만 우리는 개인주의 사회에서 살고 있다. 따라서 개인 스포츠를 잘 하면 십대들이 미래를 준비할 수 있다.